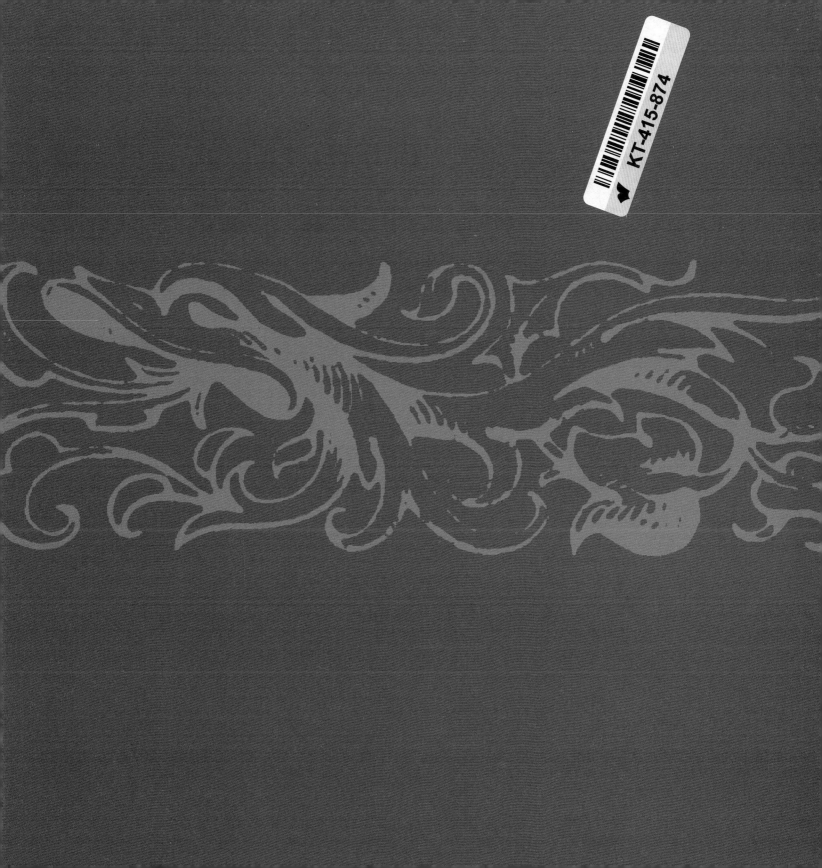

ANTONIO CARLUCCIO'S
MUSIC & MENUS FROM ITALY

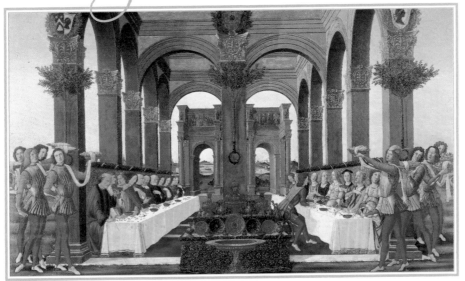

ANTONIO CARLUCCIO'S
MUSIC & MENUS FROM ITALY

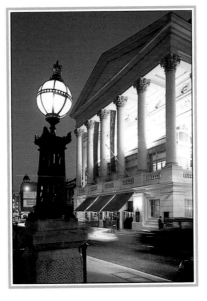

GREAT ITALIAN ARIAS
CLASSIC ITALIAN RECIPES

PAVILION

First published in Great Britain in 1996 by
Pavilion Books Limited
26 Upper Ground
London SE1 9PD

Designed by Nigel Partridge

A CIP catalogue record for this book is available from the British Library

ISBN 1-85793-529-2

Printed and bound in China by Imago

2 4 6 8 10 9 7 5 3

This book may be ordered by post direct from the publisher.
Please contact the Marketing Department. But try your bookshop first.

FRONTISPIECE: PETTO D'ANITRA AL MANGO (SEE PAGE 71)

CONTENTS

ARIAS

⚜ VERDI RIGOLETTO ⚜
LA DONNA E MOBILE 2.11
Jose Maria Perez, Tenor

The Duke of Mantua is a notorious seducer, which his hunchback jester Rigoletto finds amusing until he is tricked into assisting in the abduction of his own beloved daughter Gilda. He swears revenge, and arranges for the Duke to be lured to a remote tavern owned by the cut-throat Sparafucile. The Duke arrives, pours himself a drink and starts to sing – ironically – 'Fickle is woman fair'.

⚜ PUCCINI TOSCA ⚜
VISSI D'ARTE 2.57
Bozena Ruk-Focic, Soprano

In Puccinis dramatic opera about political and sexual power, the painter Cavaradossi, the republican lover of the singer Tosca, has fallen into the hands of Scarpia, the evil sadistic police chief. Tosca knows that in order to save his life she must submit to Scarpia's advances. In her aria 'I have lived for art, I have lived for love' the helpless Tosca gives vent to her grief.

⚜ VERDI IL TROVATORE ⚜
THE ANVIL CHORUS 2.46
Choir of the Munich State Opera

At the gypsies' camp in the mountains the troubadour Manrico, who is in fact of noble birth, is about to discover that the gypsy Azucena is not, after all, his mother. As the day's work begins, the gypsies sing a rousing chorus, swinging their hammers and striking the anvils in time with the music.

⚜ PUCCINI LA BOHEME ⚜
CHE GELIDA MANINA 3.54
Jose Maria Perez, Tenor

Rudolph, an impoverished poet, is alone in his Parisian garret on a bitterly cold Christmas Eve, and someone knocks. It is a neighbour, the consumptive Mimi, needing a light for her candle. She drops her key and, fumbling for it, their fingers touch – and he sings, 'Your tiny hand is frozen'.

⚜ ROSSINI THE BARBER OF SEVILLE ⚜
LARGO AL FACTOTUM 4.43
Tito Gobbi (Figaro)

The role of the ubiquitous Figaro, busybody, intriguer and barber to Dr Bartolo, is to help Count Almaviva to woo Rosina, the doctor's ward. In the opening scene in the street, Figaro introduces himself in an ebullient, bravura aria of rapid patter, 'Make way for the city's factotum!'

⚜ PUCCINI MADAM BUTTERFLY ⚜
UN BEL DÌ VEDREMO 4.18
Vanda Gerlovic, Soprano

Three years have passed since Butterfly's husband Lieutenant Pinkerton was recalled to America. Her maid Suzuki doubts that he will return to Nagasaki, but the trusting Butterfly, who has borne his son, is sure that he will. 'One fine day', she sings, looking forward to the day his ship reappears in the harbour and they are reunited.

⚜ PUCCINI TURANDOT ⚜
NESSUN DORMA 2.58
Eugenio Fernandi (Prince Calaf)

The Unknown Prince has successfully answered the capricious Princess Turandot's riddles, but when she still refuses to marry him he offers to die, like other unsuccessful suitors, if by morning she can discover his name. 'None shall sleep', the heralds cry, until the name is known. The Prince takes up the cry in a noble, sonorous aria, joyfully confident that the secret will be kept till dawn, when Turandot will be his.

⚜ VERDI AIDA ⚜
GRAND MARCH AND BALLET 5.43
Choir of the Munich State Opera

The story of the Ethopian slave girl Aida is one of divided loyalties, for the man she loves is Radames, who leads the Egyptian army against her people. In Act II he returns in triumph at the head of his army, with prisoners and spoils of war, as the people of Thebes sing a joyous song of victory.

VERDI RIGOLETTO
BELLA FIGLIA DELL'AMORE 4.13
Juan Perez, Tenor

Ensconced at the ramshackle tavern, the scene of his intended murder, the Duke flirts with the beautiful gypsy Maddalena ('Fairest daughter of the graces'), secretly observed from outside by the vengeful Rigoletto and the despairing Gilda, whom Rigoletto has brought to witness her seducer's infidelity. This is a magnificent quartet, in which contrasting tunes and emotions are exquisitely blended.

VERDI NABUCCO
CHORUS OF THE HEBREW SLAVES 4.19
Radio Symphony Orchestra and Choir Ljubljana/Marko Munih

Nabucco tells of the oppression of the Jews by the Assyrians, the love of Nabucco's daughter Fenena for the Jewish Ismaele and her conversion to the Hebrew faith. In Act II Scene II the enslaved Hebrews, working in chains on the banks of the Euphrates, sing a moving chorus, 'Va, pensiero', about their longed-for homeland.

VERDI LA TRAVIATA
LIBIAMO, LIBIAMO, NE' LIETI CALICI 3.10
Ernst Wiemann, Bass (Doctor of Grenvil)
William Verkerk, Tenor (Alfredo)
Choir of the Munich State Opera

Based on Dumas' La Dame aux Camélias, La Traviata tells the story of a consumptive courtesan who renounces promiscuity for love – and then, selflessly, her love. It begins with a party at Violetta's house, at which Alfredo, asked to propose a toast, leads the guests in a rousing brindisi 'Let us drink from the wine-cup overflowing'.

PUCCINI TOSCA
E LUCEVAN LE STELLE 2.42
Ricardo Casinelli, Tenor

At dawn in the Castel St Angelo, Cavaradossi awaits execution. Tosca has in fact obtained a safe conduct for the pair of them by agreeing to Scarpia's terms – before stabbing him through the heart. Believing himself to be doomed, as indeed he is, Cavaradosssi sings the lyrical aria 'When the stars were brightly shining', recalling his lost love.

BELLINI I PURITANI
SON VERGIN VEZZOSA 4.02
Luciano Pavarotti (Arturo)

Set in England during the Civil War, I Puritani tells of the love of Elvira, the daughter of a Puritan general, for the cavalier Lord Arthur Talbot. Condemned for treason, she is ultimately pardoned and celebrates in an elaborate polonaise, 'I am a blithesome maiden', in which her exultant voice soars above the other voices, chorus and orchestra.

LEONCAVALLO PAGLIACCI
VESTI LA GIUBBA 3.20
Jose Maria Perez, Tenor

Plunged into despair by the infidelity of his wide Nedda and his inability to discover the identity of her lover, Canio the strolling player sings the famous and deeply affecting aria 'On with the motley', in which he accepts the fact that, heartbroken or not, he still has to go on stage and play the clown once again.

DONIZETTI LUCIA DI LAMMERMOOR
SEXTET: CHE MI FRENA? 3.48
Luciano Pavarotti (Edgardo)

Donizetti's Scottish opera is a bleak tale of family feud and ill-fated lovers. Lucy, duped into thinking her absent lover Edgar unfaithful, is induced to marry another. Edgar's sudden appearance makes for a dramatic confrontation – 'What restrains me at this moment? Why my sword do I not straightaway draw?' – and a passionate sextet.

DONIZETTI LA FAVORITE
O MIO FERNANDO 6.40
Ruza Pospisch-Baldani, Alto

Ferdinand is unaware that Leonora, the woman he loves and who loves him, is King Alfonso's mistress. In rejecting his love she could not bring herself to reveal the true reason. Now he is a war hero, and when the King tells him to name his own reward, he asks for the hand of Leonora. The King consents, and Leonora, enraptured yet fearful about the revelation to come, sings, 'O, my Ferdinand'.

BELLINI NORMA
CASTA DIVA 5.27
Joan Sutherland (Norma)

The high point of another opera about interracial love and divided loyalties is when, in the sacred grove of the Druids, the high priestess Norma prays to Diana ('chaste goddess') for the return of her Roman lover. 'Each note,' wrote Théophile Gautier, 'suggests the sighing of the night breeze in the dewy leaves . . . an irresistibly charming effect.'

INTRODUCTION

Although my operatic singing is limited to the bathroom area, where the acoustics are particularly favourable and where one does not have to fear any criticism, I love opera and its great arias. My connection to this world started a long time ago. When I was a student in Vienna, I often had the chance to go to the Wiener Staatsoper and the Musikverein to listen to classical music. As a student I sometimes queued all night long to buy tickets to something special, and although I could only afford the cheapest, I witnessed great musical occasions with the same enthusiasm as the people in the expensive seats. I was probably having much more fun than them! Sometimes now, as I sit in comfort, I think of the people in the *piccionaia,* as they say in Italy, which means people perched like pigeons in the amphitheatre.

My interest in opera, however, remains as strong as ever. For a few years my wife and I lived in a penthouse in London in the same buildings as the Box Office of the Royal Opera House in Covent Garden. In the evening after work I could often hear rehearsals from the building opposite, and in the morning I could look straight across from our flat on the roof and see the wig-makers of the ROH at work.

The destiny which brought me in direct contact with the opera world is something I would never have dreamt of. We moved away from Covent Garden when the piazza was replaced and life became less tranquil there. In 1981, however, I took over the running of the Neal Street Restaurant, in Covent Garden which I now own. A few years later I entered into a contract with the ROH whereby my restaurant supplies the Royal Box with meals. Whoever is seated in the Royal Box may order their meal the day before the performance from a special 'take-away' menu, and it is served fresh during the intervals in a nearby dining-room. On one occasion the ROH offered me the use of the Royal Box, which I shared with some friends, and I had the unique experience of dining in that very room, with food from my own restaurant.

Being so closely connected with this establishment, I have had the pleasure of receiving a variety of operatic superstars as guests in the restaurant after a performance. The most notable visit was that of Luciano Pavarotti after his performance as Cavaradossi in *Tosca.* He came to the restaurant still wearing his costume. All the guests in the restaurant spontaneously got up to applaud this operatic giant. Placido Domingo, José Carreras, Kiri Te Kanawa, Joan Sutherland, Elizabeth Swarzkopf, Claudio Desderi, Angela Gheorghiu and many more, including conductors and dancers, have been to my restaurant over the years.

They say that art mixes well with good food; however, I believe opera is the closest to it. The idea of suggesting menus to accompany these arias struck me as a brilliant one, as good food and *belcanto* complement each other wonderfully well. I have tried to suit the food to the character of the opera and its music, sometimes relating it to the singers and sometimes to the location of the opera. I hope you will enjoy both the food and the music and ask for an encore.

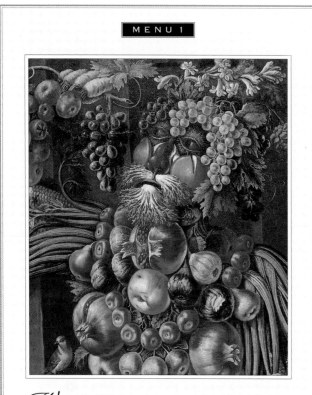

MENU 1

*W*elcome to my first menu, which has a distinctive seasonal character. This is because the first white truffles – known as *tartufi d'Alba* – appear in late October, lasting through to the end of January. The white Alba truffle is a gourmet delight, and an exceedingly expensive one at that! I call it 'food of gods, kings and pigs', as the truffles are sometimes sniffed out by pigs, although in Italy it is usually done by trained dogs. My *tagliatelle al tartuffo* always keep their high culinary promise to the customers of my restaurant. From the same region, the delicious hazelnut *torta* is a logical conclusion to the menu.

TAGLIATELLE CON TARTUFI
TAGLIATELLE WITH WHITE TRUFFLES

*O*ne of the most popular and sought after dishes in Alba is simply the combination of freshly made tagliatelle with the sophisticated rich white truffle only to be found from October through to the end of January, in the district of Piedmont. I hope you have a good friend who will give you a present of a truffle.

For this dish choose only the best Parmesan.

SERVES 4

450 g/1 lb fresh tagliatelle, preferably home-made
100 g/4 oz/½ cup unsalted butter
50 g/2 oz/½ cup freshly grated Parmesan
cheese from a newly opened parmigiano reggiano
1 small white truffle
salt and freshly ground black pepper

Cook the tagliatelle al dente. Toss in the butter and mix in the freshly grated Parmesan cheese. Season with salt and pepper. Present the tagliatelle to your guests served on separate plates. Shave the precious truffle with a 'mandolino' directly on to each serving, and you have an exceptional first course.

RIGHT: TAGLIATELLE CON TARTUFI

AGNELLO ALLA GIUDEA

LAMB WITH LEMON AND EGG

Why my mother used to call this recipe 'alla Giudea' I do not know as a similar sauce is prepared in Greece and is called avgolemono. All I know, however, was that when it was prepared with exceptionally young and tender lamb it was an exquisite dish. The same recipe can use chicken instead of lamb.

SERVES 4

600 g/1¼ lb very lean lamb (preferably from the leg),
cut into 3 cm/1¼ in pieces
4 tbsp olive oil
4 eggs
the juice of 3 medium lemons
the grated rind of 1 lemon
1 tbsp chopped parsley
2 cloves garlic, crushed to a pulp
4 tbsp stock

Heat the olive oil in a saucepan, add the pieces of lamb and brown them on all sides. When the meat is sealed, put a lid on the saucepan and reduce the heat. Cook for 15–20 minutes, shaking the pan from time to time. The resulting moisture will cook the meat.

Beat the eggs and add the lemon juice, grated rind, parsley and crushed garlic. Once the lamb is cooked, remove the saucepan from the heat, add the stock, stir well and then pour in the egg mixture. Continue to stir all the time so that the sauce thickens with the heat of the meat. Take care not to take too long as the sauce will curdle if it begins to cook.

CROCCHETTE DI PATATE AL FORMAGGIO

POTATO AND CHEESE CROQUETTES

It takes a fair bit of work to make these special favourites of my childhood. My mother always found it difficult to produce enough for the meal: she would watch us stealing them the moment they came out of the pan.

SERVES 4

600 g/1¼ lb potatoes (peeled weight)
45 g/1½ oz/3 tbsp butter
50 g/2 oz/½ cup freshly grated Parmesan cheese
2 eggs
80 g/3 oz/1¾ cups fresh breadcrumbs
4 grates of nutmeg
salt and freshly ground black pepper
oil for deep frying

Boil the potatoes in salted water until cooked, drain and mash them together with the butter and the Parmesan. Season this with freshly ground black pepper, nutmeg and salt. Beat this mixture very thoroughly and then roll into sausages 4 x 10 cm/1½ x 4 in. Lightly beat the eggs and dip the croquettes first into the egg and then roll them in breadcrumbs.

Heat the oil in a deep fryer and fry the croquettes two at a time. They should be crisp and golden on the outside. These can accompany any dish or be eaten on their own – best very hot.

TORTA DI NOCCIOLE

HAZELNUT CAKE

Hazelnut trees produce not only material for my walking sticks, but very tasty little nuts which are perfect for this cake. I like to serve this cake with a glass of Passito di Caluso or any other good dessert wine.

SERVES 6–8

125g/4½ oz/1 cup hazelnuts (shelled weight)
100 g/4 oz/½ cup butter
125 g/4½ oz/½ cup plus 2 tbsp sugar
4 large eggs, separated
25 g/1 oz/2½ tbsp flour, sifted
125 g/4½ oz/½ cup ricotta cheese
2 tsp grated lemon rind
6 tbsp peach or apricot jam mixed with 1 tbsp water
25 g/1 oz bitter chocolate

Preheat the oven to 200°C/400°F/gas mark 6. Lay the hazelnuts on a metal tray and roast them for 10 minutes in the oven – they should become a light golden colour and their skins should loosen. Let them cool, then skin them (if you shake them in a sieve, most of the skins will come off). Chop the nuts finely.

Butter a 25 cm/10 in flan tin. Soften the butter and beat it well with 70 g/3 oz/⅓ cup of the sugar. Add the egg yolks and continue to beat: the mixture should be soft and foamy. Fold in the sifted flour. In a separate bowl beat the ricotta with a fork until it is light, then add the chopped hazelnuts and the grated lemon rind.

Add this mixture to the egg yolk mixture. Beat the egg whites until they become stiff, and fold in the remaining sugar. Very carefully fold the ricotta and flour mixture into the beaten egg whites.

Spread this mixture into the flan tin and bake in the oven for 30 minutes. Let the cake cool a little, then remove from the tin and place upside down on a plate. Spread the jam mixture evenly over the top of the cake. Finely grate the bitter chocolate over the jam surface so that you have a light sprinkling all over.

RIGHT: TORTA DI NOCCIOLE

$\mathcal{T}$ypical of the northern Italian region of Lombardy, this perfect cold-weather menu features *bresaola,* the famous cured, air-dried beef of the Alpine valley of Valtellina and the classic Milanese *ossobuco,* a wonderful braise of veal marrow-bone that is usually accompanied by a *risotto alla Milanese.* Mixed sautéed wild mushrooms – for which, you may have guessed, I have a passion – match the main course perfectly, and I can think of no better way to round off the meal than a simple dessert of luscious pears baked in wine.

BRESAOLA DELLA VALTELLINA

DRIED BEEF WITH OIL AND LEMON

This antipasto is a popular dish in the Alps just north of Milan and can be compared with the German Bundnerfleisch or the Swiss viande de Grisons. The main ingredient is Bresaola, a piece of lean and tender beef silverside which has been pickled in a salt brine for 6 to 7 days and then left to stand in a well-ventilated spot for at least six months. It is usually eaten on its own (very finely machine-sliced) or with a mild dressing. In Tuscany wild boar fillet is served in the same way. A few slices added to a mixed salami antipasto will give the dish a wonderful deep red colour. The flavour of this dish is enhanced if eaten with grissini sticks.

SERVES 4

160 g/5½ oz finely sliced Bresaola
juice of 1 lemon
4 tsp olive oil
freshly ground black pepper

Arrange the Bresaola carefully and decoratively on a plate. Pour the lemon juice and olive oil over the slices and sprinkle with some freshly ground black pepper.

RIGHT: BRESAOLA DELLA VALTELLINA

OSSOBUCO MILANESE
VEAL MARROW-BONE MILANESE

This is a particularly filling dish which is usually eaten during the colder months. Of great importance is to find a butcher who will supply you with the marrow-bones or ossibuchi – so called because they are derived from the tibia of the calf which, when cut, reveals a bone with a hole filled with the marrow.

SERVES 4

4 marrow-bones (cross-cut veal shanks), 3–4 cm/1½ in thick, cut from the middle of the shin where the bone is rounded on both sides and the meat is dense
salt
flour for dusting
4 tbsp olive oil
1 small onion, sliced
1 x 400 g/14 oz can Italian peeled tomatoes, drained of half their juice
the juice and half the grated rind of 1 large orange
1 glass of dry red wine
salt and freshly ground black pepper

Dust the marrow-bones with salt and flour. Heat the olive oil in a cast-iron casserole and fry the marrow-bones two at a time on both sides, taking great care not to damage the marrow in the centre of the bone or allow it to fall out. Remove the marrow-bones from the casserole and put to one side. In the same oil, fry the onion until translucent then add the tomatoes, breaking them up in the casserole with a wooden spoon while cooking. Keep the heat up high so that the tomatoes reduce. After 5 minutes add the orange juice, the grated rind and the glass of wine. Continue to cook fast and return the marrow-bones to the sauce. Season with salt and pepper, reduce the heat, then cover and simmer for 1–1½ hours or until the meat has begun to come away from the bone. Serve with saffron rice (Risotto milanese).

FUNGHI MISTI IN UMIDO
MIXED SAUTÉED WILD MUSHROOMS

I cook this recipe every time I have had an unsuccessful mushroom hunt. I find that even the small amount of mushrooms I have gathered provide an opportunity to have a colourful, flavourful recipe, ideal to accompany autumn game dishes.

SERVES 4–6

750 g/1½ lb mixed mushrooms – oyster, field, ceps, hedgehog
1 small onion
1 large tomato
5 tbsp olive oil
2 bay leaves
1 sprig of rosemary
salt and freshly ground black pepper

Clean the mushrooms, wiping them rather than washing them if possible. Slice the onion and peel and chop the tomato. Heat the oil in a large pan, fry the onion and when it becomes golden add the tomato, the bay leaves and the sprig of rosemary. Cook the tomato for a minute or two and then add the mushrooms. Continue cooking for 20 minutes more on a low heat, stirring occasionally. Season with salt and pepper.

RIGHT: FUNGHI MISTI IN UMIDO

PERE COTTE AL FORNO

PEARS BAKED IN RED WINE

Another very easily prepared recipe using cooked pears which can be found in many Italian restaurants. My mother used to make it in autumn when pears are plentiful and when the first wine has just been pressed. She would always make more than was needed; apart from being a dessert, it was also something special for us when we returned ravenous from school. The alcohol in the wine disappears when cooked, so the pears can be given to children.

SERVES 10

10 Conference or other firm pears
1 litre/1¾ pt/1 qt dry red wine
1 cinnamon stick, 5 cm/2 in long
a few cloves
the pared rind of 1 lemon
300 g/10 oz/1½ cups sugar

Wash the pears and pack tightly, side by side, in a deep-sided ovenproof dish. Pour the wine over and add the cinnamon, cloves and lemon rind, then sprinkle half the sugar on the pears. Put into a cold oven and bring the temperature up to 200°C/400°F/gas mark 6. Cook, basting the pears every now and then with the juices. After 45 minutes sprinkle the remaining sugar on to the pears and cook for a final 10 minutes. Leave to cool before serving.

If too much liquid remains, reduce it a little by boiling it, then pour it over the pears before leaving them to cool.

*H*ere I have tried to capture some of the sunshine of southern Italy. Certainly, the wonderful locally-grown peppers and aubergines/eggplants that feature in the first course need plenty of hot sun to develop their flavours. The meat course is found all over Italy, but my version includes the aromatic rosemary that perfumes the air of the south, and nobody would dispute that the sweet *tarallucci* biscuits are typical of Naples.

Melanzane e Peperoni Ripieni

STUFFED PEPPERS AND AUBERGINES (EGGPLANTS)

*M*y mother was always good at making this recipe. I remember this dish was delicious in summer when the heat was intense. It was nearly always served cold, but still crispy on the top, and accompanied by plain bread.

Serves 4

*2 large yellow or red sweet peppers, stalks and
seeds removed
2 medium-sized aubergines (eggplants)
7 tbsp olive oil
400 g/14 oz ripe tomatoes, skinned and finely chopped
40 g/1½ oz/¼ cup finely chopped capers (salted if possible)
12 anchovy fillets
2 cloves garlic, very finely chopped
4 tbsp finely chopped parsley
80 g/3 oz/1¾ cups fresh white breadcrumbs
50 g/2 oz/½ cup freshly grated Parmesan cheese
3 grates of nutmeg
salt and freshly ground black pepper*

Preheat the oven to 200°C/400°F/gas mark 6. Slice each of the peppers and the aubergines (eggplants) in two lengthwise. Scoop out as much as you can of the flesh of the aubergine with a knife, leave the skin intact. Chop the scooped-out pulp finely and fry it in 2 tablespoons of oil for 5–6 minutes, until soft.

Chop the tomatoes, capers, anchovies, garlic and parsley finely. Then take the breadcrumbs, Parmesan and nutmeg and mix well with the chopped ingredients and the aubergine pulp, including the oil in which it was cooked. Fill the aubergine and pepper shells with this mixture. Put 2 tablespoons of oil in the bottom of an ovenproof dish and arrange them in it. Pour the remaining 3 tablespoons of oil over the stuffed vegetables and bake for around 40 minutes. Serve hot or cold.

Involtini di Carne

BEEF ROULADE

This delicious recipe may be found in all regions of Italy with a variety of different fillings and cooked in different ways. Its unchanging feature is that it must be made from thin slices of mature well-flavoured meat that can be rolled up. The topside is perhaps the most suitable meat to use. This is another extremely simple dish to prepare.

SERVES 4

4 thin slices of topside (beef round) weighing a total of
650 g/about 1½ lb
4 slices prosciutto crudo
salt and freshly ground black pepper

FOR THE FILLING:
5 small gherkin pickles or cornichons
2 tbsp chopped parsley
1 tsp chopped fresh rosemary
1 tbsp raisins

FOR THE SAUCE:
3 tbsp olive oil
1 small onion, thinly sliced
2 celery stalks, chopped
1 medium carrot, chopped
1 glass of white wine
150 ml/5 fl oz/⅔ cup stock

Beat the slices of beef with a meat-beater between sheets of plastic film as thin as you can, being careful not to break them. Spread the slices of beef out on a working surface, sprinkle them with salt and pepper and lay the slices of prosciutto on top. Finely slice the small gerkins and scatter these on to the prosciutto with the parsley, rosemary and raisins. Roll the meat up and secure each piece into a roulade with two wooden cocktail sticks.

Heat the olive oil in a cast-iron casserole and fry the roulades so that they are well browned on all sides. Remove them from the casserole and put to one side. In the same oil fry the sliced onion for a few minutes, then add the chopped celery and carrot and continue to fry, stirring from time to time, for about 10 minutes. Now pour in the glass of wine and allow it to reduce.

Return the roulades to the casserole. Add the stock, salt and pepper, cover and simmer for about 1 hour or until the meat is tender.

LEFT: INVOLTINI DI CARNE

Insalata di Finocchio

FENNEL SALAD

A bulb of fennel is a very versatile vegetable. Not only is it excellent cooked, but in its raw state it is good for every sort of salad. For those who like it, all you need do is eat it simply with good olive oil and salt and pepper. In southern Italy, little whole sweet fennel bulbs are eaten at the end of the meal instead of fruit.

SERVES 4

2 medium fennel bulbs (they must be young and fresh),
about 400 g/14 oz cleaned weight
4 tbsp virgin olive oil
salt and freshly ground black pepper

Keep a little of the green part of the fennel to scatter on the salad. Slice into very fine slices lengthwise so that each slice is held together by the stem.

Lay the slices out on a flat plate, pour over the virgin olive oil and season with salt and pepper.

RIGHT: INSALATA DI FINOCCHIO

TARALLUCCI DOLCI

SWEET TARALLUCCI

In Naples, when you say that something is going to end 'a tarallucci e vino', it means that there will be a happy ending. This could mean a row being reconciled by getting together and having a few tarallucci and some wine. I would like to see international political disputes solved in this manner. It would be very civilized indeed!

The tarallo is a ring-shaped biscuit or cookie and is usually found in many of the southern regions of Italy. It could be savoury or sweet, as in this recipe. Taralluccio is the smaller form of tarallo.

SERVES 8–10

3 medium eggs
75 g/3 oz/6 tbsp granulated sugar and 1 tbsp vanilla sugar, or a few drops
vanilla essence (extract)
1 tsp powdered cinnamon
1 tsp aniseed (optional)
2 tbsp Strega liqueur, or Anisetta
350 g/12 oz/3½ cups plain white (all-purpose) flour
1 beaten egg for sealing the rings
olive oil for frying

Beat the three eggs in a bowl with the sugar, add the cinnamon, the aniseed, the liqueur and the flour and work the mixture until you have a dough. Put it aside in a cool place covered with a cloth for 1–2 hours.

To make the tarallucci take a small piece of dough about the size of a plum and roll it into a sausage with your hands. The sausage should be about 1 cm/½ in in diameter and about 15 cm/6 in long. Form each sausage into a ring by crossing over the ends and pressing together. Seal the join with a little beaten egg.

In a small pan heat up the olive oil. The oil should be at least 2 cm/¾ in deep in the pan. Deep-fry the rings two or three at a time. Half-way through frying, after half a minute, take out the tarallucci and make an incision with a sharp knife along the top so that when you return them to the hot oil, they split open a little. Fry until golden brown, remove and drain on kitchen paper towel. Any wine is suitable to patch up a Neapolitan row!

The rustic simplicity of fresh stuffed anchovies contrasts with the more sophisticated combination of guinea fowl with pomegranate seeds. Celery is a very popular vegetable in Italy, where it is often baked or braised. Its fresh flavour makes it the perfect accompaniment to the slightly sour pomegranate sauce. Please don't ask me to explain the name of the dessert. I have no idea why it is named after a bonnet, but I can tell you that it is an authentic recipe from Piedmont!

ACCIUGHE RIPIENE AL FORNO
BAKED STUFFED ANCHOVIES

The fresh anchovy is undoubtedly one of the most popular fish in Italy. In countries where fresh anchovies are not available, it's possible to use frozen ones instead. Fresh or frozen sardines offer another alternative, but since these are larger than anchovies, you will need only half as many.

MAKES 12 'SANDWICHES'

24 fresh anchovies
1 tbsp chopped fresh dill
1 tbsp chopped fresh parsley
1 tbsp chopped fresh chives
1 tbsp chopped fresh rosemary
a few sage leaves, finely chopped
1 clove garlic, chopped
25 g/1 oz/¼ cup pine nuts, or chopped walnuts
2 tbsp olive oil
salt and freshly ground black pepper
a few drops of lemon juice
10 g/scant ½ oz/¼ cup fresh breadcrumbs

Preheat the oven to 220°C/425°F/gas mark 7. With a pair of kitchen scissors, cut off the head, tail and lower part of the fish, and discard the insides. Using your thumb, loosen the backbone from the flesh, leaving the two fillets still attached by the upper skin. Wash and dry the fish. Chop the herbs and garlic finely together and mix with the pine nuts and a tablespoon of olive oil. Grease a baking tray with a little olive oil and lay 12 of the anchovies skin side down next to each other on the tray. Spread a little of the herb mixture on each, season with salt and pepper, sprinkle with lemon juice and cover with another anchovy, skin side up, to make a 'sandwich'. Sprinkle with breadcrumbs and pour on the remaining olive oil in a thin stream. Bake for 8–10 minutes until golden. Serve hot or cold.

FARAONA AL MELOGRANO
GUINEA FOWL WITH POMEGRANATE

As they are now artificially bred, you will find no difficulty in acquiring this bird, which is a more sophisticated version of the chicken. I have chosen to prepare this dish with pomegranate, this slightly sour ingredient makes the guinea fowl all the more interesting to savour.

SERVES 4

2 guinea fowl (guinea hen) weighing 1 kg/2 lb each, with livers and giblets
2 tbsp olive oil
1 small onion
1 carrot
30 g/good 1 oz/2 tbsp butter
50 g/2 oz prosciutto crudo
1 glass of dry Marsala
1 large ripe promegranate
salt and freshly ground black pepper

Preheat the oven to 200°C/400°F/gas mark 6.

Clean the guinea fowl and brush over with a little olive oil, salt inside and out and roast in the oven for 1 hour. In the meantime, chop the onion and cut the carrot into thin slices. Heat the butter in a heavy pan and gently fry the onion and carrots. Cut the giblets and liver into small pieces, add to the frying pan, stir and fry for a few minutes before adding the sliced prosciutto. Now pour in the glass of wine and allow it to bubble for a few minutes, then turn down the flame and simmer the sauce while you peel the pomegranate. To open the pomegranate, score the skin round once and split open with your hands and take out the grains.

When the guinea fowl are cooked, remove them from the roasting pan, pour away any excess fat and deglaze with a tablespoon of water. Add to these juices the mixture and pomegranate seeds. Stir and keep hot.

Carve the breasts and legs from the birds and serve with the pomegranate sauce poured over them.

RIGHT: FARAONA AL MELOGRANO

SEDANI AL FORNO

BAKED CELERY

The intensity of the taste of baked celery wonderfully complements the flavour of game and poultry.

SERVES 4

750 g/1½ lb celery, either 1 big head or 4 smaller heads
45 g/1 ½ oz/3 tbsp butter
salt and freshly ground black pepper

Preheat the oven to 190°C/375°F/gas mark 5. Wash the celery heads and cut off the tops, leaving the young green leaves. Cut each head lengthwise in half and boil in salted water for 20–25 minutes. Drain and place the celery halves in an ovenproof dish. Pack the butter in each half, season with black pepper and bake in the oven for 15 minutes.

BONET PIEMONTESE

PIEDMONTESE BONNET

This is a typically Piedmontese dessert which, when translated, means 'cap' or bonnet. Don't ask me why. It is a richer version of crème caramel, with its distinctive burnt sugar flavour.

SERVES 6

FOR THE CAKE MIXTURE:
6 eggs
150 g/5 oz/¾ cup sugar
2 tbsp cornflour (cornstarch)
4 tbsp unsweetened cocoa powder
400 ml/14 fl oz/1¾ cups double (heavy) cream
600 ml/1 pt/2½ cups milk
15 crumbled amaretti biscuits (cookies)
a small glass dark rum – about 4 tbsp

FOR THE CARAMEL:
50 g/2 oz/¼ cup sugar
2 tbsp water

Preheat the oven to 160°C/325°F/gas mark 3.

To make the cake mixture, whisk the eggs, the sugar, the cornflour (cornstarch) and cocoa until creamy. Add the cream, the milk, crumbled amaretti and the rum and mix. To make the caramel, put the sugar and water in a pan and heat until the sugar dissolves and changes colour. Pour the caramelized sugar into the bottom of individual soufflé dishes. Pour the cake mixture on top and put them in the oven in a dish filled with water. Bake at a low heat for about 1 hour. Remove, cool and put in the refrigerator for 2–3 hours. Turn upside down on to plates and serve with more amaretti biscuits (cookies).

*A*s I am something of a mushroom fanatic, my restaurant is a mecca for people who come from far and wide to enjoy the many ways in which we cook fungi. In fact, there are also a number of ways to stuff mushrooms, and a wealth of suitable varieties, especially the caps of the porcini mushrooms we Italians prize so highly. For the first course you can use the large, flat caps of cultivated mushrooms. *Cotechino* sausage with lentils is another classic Italian speciality. You will like the speed and simplicity of my version of *tiramisu,* which will conclude the menu perfectly.

FUNGHI RIPIENI
STUFFED MUSHROOMS

*F*or this recipe you can use open cultivated mushrooms or field mushrooms. The stuffing need not be exactly as I suggest, but can be diversified according to your imagination and to the ingredients at hand.

SERVES 4

4 large open mushrooms
1 egg
1 small ripe tomato, skinned and chopped
25 g/1 oz/about 1 large slice fresh bread
4 tbsp freshly grated Parmesan cheese
1 clove garlic, chopped
1 tbsp finely chopped parsley
salt and freshly ground black pepper
3 tsp olive oil
1 tbsp dry breadcrumbs

Preheat the oven to 220°C/425°F/gas mark 7. Clean the mushrooms. Detach the stalks and chop them coarsely. Prepare the filling: first beat the egg and add to it the chopped mushroom stalks, the chopped tomato, the roughly broken up bread, the Parmesan, chopped garlic, parsley, salt and pepper and finally 1 tsp olive oil. Mix well together and fill the mushroom cups with the mixture. Oil a baking dish and on it place the mushrooms side by side. Sprinkle the dry breadcrumbs over the mushrooms and trickle with a little olive oil. Bake in the oven for 20 minutes until golden brown on top. Eat hot or cold.

RIGHT: FUNGHI RIPIENI

Cotechino con Lenticchie

SAUSAGE WITH LENTILS

The sausage or 'cotechino' is a typical speciality from Modena. I suggest that you cook the lentils separately and that you add them to the sausage at the end.

SERVES 4

1 cotechino sausage weighing about 600 g/1¼ lb
400 g/14 oz lentils (large brown type)
2 cloves garlic
3 tbsp olive oil
1 x 400 g/14 oz can peeled plum tomatoes
good pinch of dried oregano
salt and freshly ground black pepper

Put a large saucepan of water on to boil. In a separate saucepan, simmer the lentils in plenty of salted boiling water for 15 minutes.

Slice the cloves of garlic. In a large pan heat the olive oil and briefly fry the garlic; the moment it begins to change colour, add the tomatoes. Roughly break up the tomatoes as they fry in the pan. Cook over a medium flame for 10 minutes, reducing the tomatoes to a sauce. At this point put the sausage in the large saucepan of boiling water and simmer for 30 minutes. When the lentils are cooked, drain them well and add to the tomatoes and garlic in the pan; season with salt and pepper and oregano. Stir well and continue to cook for a further 10 minutes, testing the lentils, which should not be reduced to a mush but retain a 'bite'.

Serve the sausage, sliced into slices 1 cm/½ in thick, with the lentils and possibly some mostarda di Cremona. A wonderful winter dish.

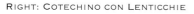

RIGHT: COTECHINO CON LENTICCHIE

PURÉ DI CAROTE E SEDANO RAPA

CARROT AND CELERIAC PURÉE

This is a speciality of my restaurant and judging by the number of times it is asked for, it seems to be popular.

SERVES 4

300 g/10 oz celeriac (peeled weight)
300 g/10 oz carrots (peeled weight)
3 tbsp double (heavy) cream
4 grates of nutmeg
salt and freshly ground black pepper

Slice the celeriac into 2 cm/¾ in thick slices; cut each carrot lengthwise into four. Boil together in salted water for 20 minutes. They should be soft. Drain and put them through a mouli while they are still hot. Add the cream, grated nutmeg and salt and pepper.

TIRAMI SU

PICK-ME-UP

This is one of my favourite desserts made from that killer of a cheese – mascarpone. There are many recipes for Tirami Su, which translated means 'pick me up' or 'lift me up', due obviously to the large amount of calories in it! I developed this recipe using only a few ingredients. The result is stunning, judging by the reaction of the customers in my restaurant.

SERVES 4

1 egg yolk
1 tbsp sugar
1 tsp vanilla sugar
250 g/9 oz mascarpone cheese
170 ml/6 fl oz/¾ cup strong black coffee
1 tbsp coffee liqueur (Kahlua)
10–12 Savoiardi biscuits (cookies)
1–2 tbsp unsweetened cocoa powder

Put the egg yolk, sugar and vanilla sugar in a bowl and mix gently to a creamy consistency. Add the mascarpone and fold in to obtain a cream. Put the coffee in a bowl with the coffee liqueur. Dip the biscuits (cookies) for a second or two in the coffee mixture, letting them absorb just enough to keep firm but not all fall apart. Starting with the biscuits, arrange in four individual dishes alternating layers of biscuit and mascarpone, ending with mascarpone. Dust with cocoa powder and put into the fridge to set and chill.

The marvellous seafood caught in Italian waters is the principal feature in this rather sophisticated, colourful menu, appearing in the first course and then in the main course. The fish risotto is a speciality of Venice; try to use a *superfino* or round-grained Italian rice of good quality such as Vialone Nano or Carnaroli, which will produce the right creaminess.

For the main course try to find fresh, raw Mediterranean prawns/shrimps, which are superior by far to the more commonly available cooked ones. The dessert is not a classic Italian dish at all, but one that I created for my restaurant.

RISOTTO NERO
BLACK RISOTTO

This typically Venetian dish has an exceptional taste and is invariably to be found on the menu of all the renowned restaurants in Venice. Use small cuttlefish, as the bigger ones are tougher.

SERVES 4

500 g/1 lb cuttlefish, to make 300 g/10 oz when cleaned
2 tbsp olive oil and 30 g/1 oz/2 tbsp butter for frying
1 small onion, chopped
half a glass of white wine
350 g/12 oz/2 cups Arborio rice
1.5 litres/3 pt/1½ qt fish stock
a generous nut of butter
salt and freshly ground black pepper

Clean the cuttlefish: first pull off the head with the tentacles, then pull out the rest of the contents of the body, which is bag-shaped. Take out the backbone and remove the outside skin from the bag, which should end up white. Among the contents of the body, find the small sac containing the ink (a bluish-silver colour) and put it to one side. Discard the mouth, shaped like a small ball and situated in the middle of the tentacles, and the eyes, which are on the top of the head. Wash and then slice the tentacles and body into 1 cm/½ in pieces.

Heat the oil and butter for frying, add the chopped onion and cook gently until translucent. Then add the cut-up cuttlefish and continue to fry for 10 minutes, until the cuttlefish has coloured. Add the wine to the pan and cook for another 5 minutes. Now pour in the rice, then gradually add the simmering fish stock, about a ladle at a time, stirring constantly.

When the rice is nearly ready, add the ink from the cuttlefish sac to the last ladle of stock and stir into the rice. Finish cooking and remove from the fire. Add the remaining nut of butter, salt and pepper to taste, and serve hot.

GAMBERONI AGLIO, OLIO E PEPERONCINO

PRAWNS (SHRIMP) IN GARLIC, OIL AND CHILLI SAUCE

Two main advantages are obtained by cooking these prawns together with oil and other ingredients: firstly the delicious juice from the prawns will flavour the broth; secondly the chilli, garlic and oil will flavour the prawn meat. The best way of appreciating to the full this inter-reaction is to mop up the sauce with some good bread. With this dish, one's hands prove to be even more useful instruments than either a spoon or fork.

For this recipe you should try and obtain some of those famous red and fleshy prawns, which I came across once in a market in Salerno. An ideal wine to accompany this dish is a good, young red wine, served chilled.

SERVES 4

12 tbsp olive oil
2 whole dried red chilli peppers, crumbled
5 or 6 large whole prawns (jumbo shrimp) per person
4 cloves garlic, chopped fine

Heat the olive oil in a pan, add the crumbled chillies and then immediately the prawns. Fry, turning the prawns over frequently, for 2 minutes. Now add the chopped garlic and allow the flavour to seep into the prawns – this will take only a few seconds. Serve the prawns in warmed individual terracotta bowls. Accompany them with some good bread to dip into the flavoured oil.

INSALATA DI CAROTE E CORIANDOLO

CARROT AND CORIANDER SALAD

The carrot has a multitude of uses and is excellent raw as long as it is sliced finely. For this reason it is better to use large but young juicy carrots. Coriander used to be a frequently used kitchen herb and there seems to be a revival in the use of herbs like these. It is easily found in Greek and Indian stores.

SERVES 4

4 large carrots, peeled (peeled weight about 400 g/14 oz)
small bunch fresh coriander (cilantro) to yield about 3 tbsp of leaves
the juice of 1 lemon
4 tbsp olive oil
salt and freshly ground black pepper

Grate the carrots on the largest-sized grater so that you get long strips of carrot. Remove the stalks from the coriander (cilantro). Mix together and dress with lemon juice, salt, olive oil and ground black pepper just before serving.

LEFT: GAMBERONI AGLIO, OLIO E PEPERONCINO

MANGO ALLO SCIROPPO DI LIMO
MANGO IN LIME SYRUP

This is an exception to my rule of using only fruit in season. The mango, an excellent exotic fruit, is obviously imported from the Far East or Brazil. Unfortunately, it is picked while still green in order to keep it fresh during transport. Even so, some mangoes have an excellent flavour even when ripened in the packing case. The smaller Brazilian type is exquisite. But don't use canned ones.

SERVES 4

2 limes
100 g/4 oz/½ cup sugar
2 tbsp water
2 ripe mangoes, or 4 if they are small ones
4 or 8 fresh mint leaves

Pare the rind of the limes and slice the rind lengthwise into very thin strips. Squeeze the juice and put this in a pan with the sugar. Add the water and heat for a few minutes until reduced to a syrup. Towards the end of this process, add the lime rind, mix to coat with the syrup and allow to cool.

Peel the mangoes with a very sharp knife. Cut them lengthwise as close as possible to the stone, which is flat, to obtain two caps. Slice these across the other way and, taking care to keep them together, arrange on a plate. Pour the syrup over including the strips of rind and decorate with mint before serving.

RIGHT: MANGO ALLO SCIROPPO DI LIMO

*T*his is one of my favourite menus, and all the dishes are long-established items on my menu. The soup is the most delicious imaginable, and you will not be surprised to see that it includes, once again, my beloved porcini mushrooms. If you can't get the fresh wild fungi, dried porcini are generally available and may be combined very successfully with cultivated mushrooms. The chicken supremes were served at a lunch hosted by a food company which awarded a prize for my first book, *An Invitation to Italian Cooking,* and the dish is very simple to prepare. The lemony chicken, sharpened with capers, is wonderfully complemented by the sweet stewed peppers, a speciality of Piedmont. So for that matter is the superb dessert of baked peaches stuffed with crumbled *amaretti,* egg yolks and pine nuts.

CREMA DI PORCINI
CREAM OF CEP SOUP

*T*his is one of the most delicious soups that I have ever created, and extremely popular in my restaurant.

During the season I use only fresh porcini, but I also deep-freeze large numbers of these delicacies in order to guarantee a plentiful supply when out of season. They keep so well that after thawing, they can even be sautéed when required, although a short cut in soup-making is simply to add the frozen mushrooms to the boiling stock.

SERVES 4

500 g/1 lb fresh Boletus edulis, *or alternatively 500 g/1 lb cultivated champignons plus 25 g/1 oz dried ceps*
1 medium onion, finely chopped
4 tbsp olive oil
1 litre/1¾ pt/1 qt beef stock
4 tbsp double (heavy) cream
salt and freshly ground pepper

FOR THE CROÛTONS
a nut of butter
2 slices white bread

If you are using fresh ceps, clean them and cut them into pieces. Cook the onion in the oil for 3–4 minutes, then add the ceps and sauté them for 6–7 minutes. Add the stock, bring to the boil and simmer for 20 minutes. (If you are using dried ceps soak them in lukewarm water for 10 minutes. Meanwhile, fry the field mushrooms together with the onions and then add the soaked ceps with their water and the stock. Simmer for about half an hour.)

To finish either method, take the pan from the heat and blend the contents. Return the soup to the pan, add the cream, salt and pepper and heat slowly. To make croûtons, cut the bread into little cubes and fry in butter.

SUPREME DI POLLO AL LIMONE
CHICKEN SUPREME WITH CAPERS AND LEMON

Chicken meat is very delicate and is suitable for almost any diet. This way of cooking it contrasts the tenderness of the breast with the intense flavour of the capers and the acidity of the lemon. This is an extremely easy recipe, and chicken breasts can be found anywhere.

SERVES 4

4 chicken breasts (breast halves)
white flour for dusting
salt and freshly ground black pepper
1 tbsp capers (salted if possible)
45 g/1½ oz/3 tbsp butter
the grated rind and juice of 1 large lemon

Season the flour with salt and pepper and roll the chicken breasts lightly in it. Put the capers to soak in a little water.

Heat the butter in a large pan and when it is hot, not brown, add the chicken breasts. Fry gently on each side until they are cooked and golden brown – about 15 minutes. Remove the chicken to a heated serving dish. Now add to the same pan the capers (chopped into pieces if they are the large variety), the grated rind of the lemon and all its juice. Stir well to deglaze the pan, season with salt and pepper and pour over the chicken.

PEPERONATA
STEWED PEPPERS

This is a typically Piedmontese dish based on peppers, tomatoes, onions and celery.

SERVES 4

1 medium-sized onion
2 large red sweet peppers
2 celery stalks, with leaves
4 ripe tomatoes
5 tbsp olive oil
salt and freshly ground black pepper

Prepare the vegetables; chop the onion, dice the red peppers, slice the celery and skin and roughly chop the tomatoes. Heat the oil in a large frying pan. When hot fry the onion, and as it begins to turn in colour add the peppers and celery. Fry together for 2 or 3 minutes. Now add the tomatoes and turn the heat down so that you slowly simmer the vegetables until they are reduced and resemble a ratatouille. This may take 35–40 minutes. Season with salt and pepper and serve either hot or cold.

PESCHE RIPIENE AL FORNO

BAKED STUFFED PEACHES

A typical recipe from Piedmont where the peaches grow in abundance. For this recipe you need those lovely big ripe peaches with the yellow flesh. This dish can be made well in advance as baked peaches are excellent cold, but not straight from the fridge.

SERVES 4

4 ripe peaches
2 tbsp unsweetened cocoa powder
4 amaretti biscuits (cookies), crumbled
2 egg yolks
2 tbsp sugar plus 2 or 3 drops vanilla, or 2 tbsp vanilla sugar
1 tbsp pine nuts

Preheat the oven to 200°C/400°F/gas mark 6. Cut the peaches in two and remove the stones.

Scoop out some of the flesh from the middle of the peaches to make room for the filling. Mix the cocoa with the crumbled biscuits (cookies), the egg yolks, sugar, vanilla and pine nuts, blending well. Fill the cavities of the peaches with this mixture. Grease an ovenproof dish and put the peaches in it. Bake for 15–20 minutes. This excellent dessert needs a glass of Moscato d'Asti to go with it.

LEFT: PEPERONATA

*T*his mouthwatering menu celebrates the warmth and *al fresco* feeling of early summer, when the fresh tender vegetables for the pasta, the young leaf spinach accompaniment and the strawberries for the tart are all cheap and plentiful. The tender little quails are available all year round. Raisins soaked in *grappa* make a very suitable sauce for these delicious birds.

TAGLIOLINI PRIMAVERA
SPRING TAGLIOLINI

*W*hy I persist in calling this dish 'spring' tagliolini is a mystery even to me, as most of the herbs involved are to be found throughout the summer months.

Ideally you should use home-made tagliolini, but commercially bought 'paglia e fieno' can prove satisfactory.

SERVES 4

400 g/14 oz paglia e fieno, or 450 g/1 lb fresh pasta dough
2 tbsp chopped fresh mint
2 tbsp chopped fresh coriander (cilantro)
2 tbsp chopped fresh parsley
1 tbsp chopped fresh dill
1 tbsp chopped sage
2 tbsp chopped fresh basil
30 g/good 1 oz/6 tbsp pine nuts, chopped
2 tbsp olive oil
100 g/4 oz/½ cup butter
1 clove garlic, finely chopped
30 g/good 1 oz/¼ cup freshly grated Parmesan cheese
salt and freshly ground black pepper

Roll out the pasta dough and cut it into tagliolini – the thinnest of pasta ribbons. Make a paste by chopping together on a board all the herbs, the nuts, and mixing in the oil. In a pan melt the butter and add the chopped garlic.

Boil the pasta in salted water; the dried variety will take 5 minutes, the home-made sort 3 minutes. Drain, retaining a little of the cooking water. At this point, mix the garlic and butter in with the herb paste and the Parmesan cheese, season with salt and pepper, and add a drop of the hot pasta water to make the sauce a more creamy consistency.

Thoroughly mix the paste into the pasta, taste for seasoning, and serve on warm plates.

TAGLIOLINI PRIMAVERA

Quaglie con Uvetta alla Grappa

QUAILS WITH GRAPPA RAISINS

A little planning is necessary for this dish, as you should put some raisins to soak in the grappa a couple of days beforehand. (Unless, of course, you have some already made. This is extremely simple: all you need is a jar filled with seedless raisins and topped up with grappa.)

Quails are easy to find all the year round as they are now bred for consumption. They represent a light but elegant dish for people without much appetite.

Serves 4

50 g/2 oz/⅓ cup seedless raisins, soaked in a small glass of grappa
8 plucked quails
salt and freshly ground black pepper
2 tbsp olive oil
45 g/1½ oz/3 tbsp butter
3–4 tbsp stock
1 tbsp chopped parsley

Put the raisins to soak in a small glass of grappa, two or three days ahead.

Preheat the oven to 200°C/400°F/gas mark 6. Clean the quails thoroughly, and rub with salt and pepper both inside and out. Heat the olive oil in a heavy pan or casserole over a strong flame, and fry the quails until they become golden on all sides: this will only take a few minutes. Place the open casserole into the hot oven and bake the birds for a further 10 minutes. When the quails are cooked, remove them from the casserole and keep them warm. Skim away any excess oil. Put the casserole back on a high flame, add the butter and with a wooden spoon stir it into the juices. Remove the raisins and add the grappa to the quail juices and butter in the pan; allow to evaporate for a minute, then add the stock, stir to deglaze the quail juices and now add the raisins and the chopped parsley. Season with salt and pepper and pour over the quails.

SPINACI, OLIO E LIMONE

SPINACH WITH OIL AND LEMON

This is one of the best ways of using an oil and lemon dressing. The oil gives a certain softness, and the sharpness of the lemon brings out the flavour of the vegetables.

SERVES 4

600 g/1¼ lb washed spinach
3 tbsp olive oil (virgin if possible)
the juice of ½ lemon
salt and freshly ground black pepper

Wash the spinach thoroughly and leave whole. In a large saucepan put water up to 5 cm/2 in deep, add salt and bring to the boil. When boiling, add the spinach, cook for 2 minutes or less if the spinach is very tender, drain immediately and pour over it the oil mixed with the juice of half a lemon. Freshly ground black pepper is excellent added to the dressing.

CROSTATA DI FRAGOLE

STRAWBERRY TART

This tart is wonderful when made with freshly gathered wild strawberries. Alternatively, any fruits such as blueberries, blackberries and raspberries are delicious made into this type of fresh fruit tart.

SERVES 6–8

700 g/1½ lb fresh strawberries
100 ml/3½ fl oz/7 tbsp water
the juice of ½ lemon
150 g/5 oz/¾ cup sugar
4 leaves gelatine (or equivalent amount of powdered gelatine)

FOR THE PASTRY:
250 g/9 oz/1⅔ cups flour
50 g/2 oz/¼ cup sugar
a pinch of salt
100 g/4 oz/½ cup unsalted butter
4 tbsp dry sherry

To make the pastry, sift together the flour, sugar and salt, add the butter cut into small pieces and mix together with your finger-tips until the butter has completely crumbled. Add the sherry and mix lightly to make a dough. Cover and put aside in a cool place for at least an hour. Preheat the oven to 175°C/350°F/gas mark 4.

Roll out the pastry and line a tart tin 25 cm/10 in in diameter. Prick the surface and bake blind for 15–20 minutes or until the pastry is cooked.

Wash the strawberries and choose 180 g/7 oz of the least good-looking ones. Cut into slices and put them in a small saucepan with the water, the juice of half a lemon, and the sugar. Bring to the boil and boil until the juice takes on some colour and becomes slightly syrupy. Remove from the heat, stir in the gelatine and leave to cool a little. Meanwhile, slice the remainder of the strawberries and sprinkle with a little lemon juice, keeping one beautiful strawberry aside for decoration. When the pastry and the strawberry syrup have cooled, spread a layer of the jellied syrup over the bottom of the tart case. Arrange the fresh cut strawberries overlapping each other in a decorative way to make concentric circles. Place the whole uncut strawberry in the centre. Leave it to set before serving.

CROSTATA DI FRAGOLE

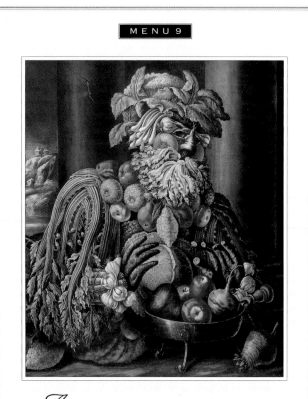

A classic Italian menu with an inter-regional character. The *vitello tonnato,* originally from the north is found virtually everywhere, and I have added my own special touch to the recipe. The *parmigiana di melanzana* comes from Campania, where the best buffalo-milk mozzarella is made, and has become popular throughout Italy. In my version I use *fontina* cheese instead of the rather chewy, commonly available cows' milk mozzarella, for a softer texture. The rich ricotta tart is similar to the kind my mother used to make for special occasions, but probably originated in the south.

VITELLO TONNATO

VEAL IN TUNA FISH SAUCE

*T*his is rather an unusual combination of meat and fish, but which results in a very tasty dish. It is popular in all regions of Italy – perhaps the Piedmontese version is the easiest of all to make. My idea of incorporating the chopped vegetables which have been cooked in the meat broth, I think, adds some extra interest to this dish. The cut of veal used in Italy is the 'girello' or eye of silverside which provides very fine, close-textured slices when cut across the grain.

SERVES 12 OR MORE

a piece of veal steak weighing about 1 kg/2 lb
1 carrot, chopped
some celery stalks, cut in pieces
1 onion
170 g/6 oz tuna fish in oil
2 tbsp capers, plus a few extra for decoration
6 anchovy fillets
150 g/5 oz/²⁄₃ cup fresh mayonnaise
a dozen or so gherkin pickles or cornichons for decoration
salt and freshly ground black pepper

Boil the meat together with the pieces of carrot, celery and onion and a pinch of salt for around 1 hour. Leave to cool, then cut into very thin slices and arrange on a dish. Put the vegetables together with the tuna, capers and anchovies through the food processor to produce a smooth paste, the consistency of thick cream, which can then be incorporated into the mayonnaise. Add salt and pepper, spread the paste over the veal slices and decorate with gherkins and capers.

Insalata di Fagiolini alla Menta

FRENCH (GREEN) BEAN SALAD WITH MINT

What could be simpler than green beans in a salad? This recipe can be eaten either hot or cold. It is important to have very fresh beans, without strings. The combination of the garlic and mint, along with the oil and lemon, gives a totally unexpected flavour.

SERVES 4

320 g/12 oz cleaned French (green) beans
salt
3 sprigs of mint
1 clove garlic
4 tbsp olive oil
the juice of 1 lemon
freshly ground black pepper

Top and tail the beans. Boil them in plenty of salted water until quite tender. Drain. Finely chop the mint and the garlic. Then mix them with the oil, lemon juice, salt and pepper and stir into the beans. Mix well and eat hot or cold.

La Parmigiana di Melanzane

TIMBALE OF AUBERGINES (EGGPLANTS)

I've never known whether this dish is called parmigiana because it comes from Parma, or because it's made with Parmesan cheese. The aubergines (eggplants) should be nice and firm, with not too many seeds. I use fontina cheese instead of mozzarella, as good mozzarella which remains soft when cooked is hard to find outside Italy. Another of my variations is to coat the aubergine slices in flour and egg before frying: I've discovered that in this way they absorb less oil, and even with the egg, are lighter and tastier. A good result is obtained by using courgettes (zucchini) in place of aubergines.

SERVES 6 AS A MAIN COURSE OR 10–12 AS A STARTER

4 large aubergines (eggplants) weighing altogether 1–1½ kg/about 2½ lb
salt
flour for coating
4 eggs
plenty of olive oil for frying

FOR THE SAUCE:
1½ x 400 g cans peeled plum tomatoes
4 tbsp olive oil
1 clove garlic, chopped
10 fresh basil leaves
salt and freshly ground black pepper
300 g/10 oz fontina cheese
100 g/4 oz/freshly grated Parmesan cheese

Slice the aubergines about 1 cm/½ in thick. Sprinkle the slices with salt and put them to stand for half an hour stacked one on top of the other with a weight on top, so that their juice can drain away. Wipe the slices dry and dust them on both sides in flour. Beat the eggs, season with salt, dip the floured aubergine slices into the egg, then fry 3 or 4 at a time in hot oil. Brown on both sides, remove and drain on kitchen paper towel. This is a slow process so allow plenty of time. Chop the tomatoes with their juices in the can. Heat the olive oil in a large pan and gently fry the garlic, allow it to colour but not brown. Add the tomatoes and cook for 15 minutes, adding salt, pepper and the basil leaves towards the end. Slice the fontina cheese. Preheat the oven to 200°C/400°F/gas mark 6.

Put two or three spoonfuls of tomato sauce in the bottom of a large ovenproof dish, then arrange a layer of the aubergine slices. Cover the aubergines with some pieces of fontina cheese, spoon a little tomato sauce on the cheese and then add a sprinkling of Parmesan. Continue arranging them in the opposite direction to the layer below. The final layer should be of tomato sauce dotted with fontina and a generous amount of Parmesan. Bake in the oven for 25–30 minutes. Leave the dish to sit for 15 minutes before cutting up to serve.

RIGHT: LA PARMIGIANA DI MELANZANE

CROSTATA DI RICOTTA

RICOTTA TART

This tart is a cheese-based dessert with a superb result which my mother used to make from time to time as a special treat, usually on a Sunday. Ricotta is used all over Italy to make sweets. However, the ingredients and method suggest that this recipe comes from the south.

SERVES 10

FOR THE PASTRY:
100 g/4 oz/½ cup unsalted butter
50 g/2 oz/¼ cup sugar
4 tbsp dry sherry
a pinch of salt
250 g/9 oz/1⅔ cups flour

FOR THE FILLING:
40 g/1½ oz candied orange peel
40 g/1½ oz candied lemon peel
40 g/1½ oz candied angelica
40 g/1½ oz bitter sweet chocolate
2 egg yolks
150 g/5 oz/¾ cup caster (superfine) sugar
pared rind of ½ lemon, chopped
500 g/1 lb/2½ cups very fresh ricotta

For the pastry, work the butter with the sugar, sherry and salt to a smooth consistency. Add the flour and work to obtain a stiffish dough. Put aside, covered, in a cool place for 1 hour.

The candied peel, angelica and chocolate should all be chopped into very small pieces about 5 mm/¼ in square. Beat the egg yolks with the sugar until creamy, add the chopped lemon rind. Beat the ricotta with a fork until light, then add to the egg mixture. Stir in the candied peel and chocolate pieces.

Preheat the oven to 190°C/375°F/gas mark 5. Line the bottom and sides of a cake tin with three-quarters of the pastry. Pour in the ricotta mixture and spread it evenly. Roll out the rest of the pastry and cut into strips 2 cm/¾ in wide. Make a lattice top on the tart. Put in the oven and bake until the top starts to turn brown – about 30–40 minutes. Serve cold.

$\mathcal{W}$ild mushroom risotto is another northern speciality to which I am addicted. As always, you can use a combination of dried porcini mushrooms and fresh cultivated mushrooms, but nothing beats the flavour of the fresh wild porcini that traditionally go into this risotto. The spare-ribs are very rustic in character, and are well matched by the earthy baked artichokes and potatoes. After so much gutsy food, a delicate sorbet flavoured with *dragoncello* (tarragon) is a superb way to finish the meal.

RISOTTO CON PORCINI
WILD MUSHROOM RISOTTO

This is the wild mushroom recipe I cook most often. It is, in my view, the most satisfying dish.

SERVES 4

300–350 g/about 12 oz firm, small fresh ceps, or fresh button
mushrooms plus 25 g/1 oz dried ceps (soaked)
1 small onion, finely chopped
2 tbsp olive oil
30 g/1 oz/2 tbsp butter
350 g/12 oz/2 cups/Arborio rice
1.5 litres/3 pt/1½ qt hot chicken stock or water plus
2 bouillon cubes
salt and freshly ground black pepper

TO FINISH:
a nut of butter
60 g/2 oz/½ cup freshly grated Parmesan cheese

Slice the fresh mushrooms. Fry the onion in the oil and butter; when it begins to colour, add the sliced mushrooms and continue to fry over a moderate flame for a couple of minutes. If using the dried ceps, chop them into small pieces and add to the fresh mushrooms, keeping the water they soaked in to add to the risotto later with the stock.

Add the rice to the pan and stir with a wooden spoon until it is well coated with oil and butter. Add about a ladleful of stock to the rice at a time (have the stock simmering in a pan next to the risotto), stirring continually with a wooden spoon. As the rice grains absorb the liquid, add more. Continue to stir and add the stock until the rice is cooked – about 20–25 minutes.

When the rice is 'al dente', remove from the heat, season, and finish by stirring in the nut of butter and the Parmesan cheese. Serve hot and, if you like, decorate each portion with a slice of mushroom.

Costine di Maiale con Ceci

PORK SPARE-RIBS WITH CHICK PEAS

Here is another rustic pork recipe which – although it could never feature as nouvelle cuisine – is tasty enough to be appreciated by even the most delicate of palates.

SERVES 4

1 kg/2lb pork spare-ribs with plenty of meat on them
250 g/8 oz dried chick peas, or 2 medium cans of chick peas
3 tbs olive oil
5 cloves garlic, chopped
2 stalks of celery, chopped
2 carrots, chopped
1 x 400 g can Italian peeled plum tomatoes
salt and freshly ground black pepper
a little stock (optional)
5 or 6 fresh basil leaves

Put the dried chick peas to soak in a lot of water (remember they will increase their volume threefold) for 24 hours. Strain the chick peas and add to a saucepan of boiling salted water. Boil gently for 1½ hours or until they are cooked al dente.

Take a thick-bottomed saucepan or casserole large enough to contain both the meat and the chick peas. Heat the olive oil in this pan and thoroughly brown the spare-ribs: this will take at least 15 minutes. Move the spare-ribs around in the pan so that they do not stick. Chop the garlic, the celery and the carrots and add to the spare-ribs. Fry very briefly, just coating the vegetables with oil, and then add the tomatoes and all their juice and season with salt and pepper. Cook the spare-ribs in the tomato sauce for about 20 minutes, then add the drained chick peas. If there is not sufficient liquid in the pan to cover the spare-ribs and the chick peas, add a ladle of stock or tomato juice.

Cover the pan and simmer for 45 minutes or until the spare-ribs are cooked: the meat should be coming away from the bones. Add the basil leaves 5 minutes before serving. Home-made bread, as usual, is a good accompaniment to this wholesome dish.

RIGHT: COSTINE DI MAIALE CON CECI

Carciofi e Papate al Forno

BAKED ARTICHOKES AND POTATOES

Only small tender artichokes, which unfortunately are rarely seen in markets outside Italy, are suitable for this recipe. If you must use the bigger ones, make sure to remove all the hard bits which, even when cooked, contain tough threads. It is possible to use artichokes that seem too old for boiling, since all but the centre is peeled away. It is an ideal dish for vegetarians.

Serves 4

50 g/2 oz/⅓ cup capers (salted if possible)
350 g/12 oz potatoes (peeled weight)
250 g/8 oz artichokes (peeled weight)
a slice of lemon
1 medium-sized onion
5 tbsp olive oil
100 ml/3½ fl oz/7 tbsp stock
25 g/1 oz/⅔ cup fresh breadcrumbs
salt and freshly ground black pepper

Preheat the oven to 190°C/375°F/gas mark 5. Put the capers to soak in a small bowl of water. Peel and slice the potatoes 5 mm/¼ in thick. Wash the artichokes, pull off the tough leaves, cut away the top, slice into quarters (or eighths if they are big artichokes) and remove any choke from the centre. Put aside in a bowl of cold water with a slice of lemon in it. Slice the onion finely. Grease an ovenproof dish with olive oil, then make alternating layers of potato, onion and artichoke. Sprinkle each layer with a few capers, salt and pepper. Pour in the stock, cover the top with breadcrumbs and trickle with olive oil. Cover the dish with foil and bake in the oven for 40 minutes. Remove the foil and bake for a further 20 minutes until crisp and golden on top. Serve at once.

SORBETTO AL DRAGONCELLO

TARRAGON FRUIT SORBET

It is possible to produce any sort of ice cream or sorbet manually with the aid of a deep freeze. The trick is to turn a mixture of fruit juice or flavoured milk and the correct amount of sugar into a crystallized mass fluffy enough to be easily spooned. Care should be taken to whisk the ingredients just before they solidify to break down the crystals. This can be done by keeping an eye on the state of the sorbet or ice cream after an hour or so in the freezer. After whisking the mixture for a few seconds, it should be returned to the freezer. Nowadays, a sorbetiére or ice cream machine will do all this for you.

This is my newest recipe. I hope you like it.

SERVES 4

2 tbsp finely chopped fresh tarragon leaves
300 g/10 oz/1½ cups sugar
750 ml/1¼ pt/3 cups water
the juice of 2 large lemons

Boil together the tarragon, sugar, water and lemon juice for 2–3 minutes just to blend the flavour of the tarragon into the sugar. Cool the syrup, put in the freezer and proceed as described in the introduction.

MENU 11

A slightly unusual menu with more dishes from my restaurant. As an Italian, naturally I love seafood, and I can think of no better way to enjoy succulent *frutti di mare* than to serve them in a salad. My customers seem to agree with me. Follow this with the sweet-and-sour main course accompanied by broccoli with garlic and ginger, and finish off with the elaborate and remarkable tart, made with whole wheat, eggs, ricotta, sugar, spice, lemon zest and candied peel. This is rather rich but a small slice is sufficient to settle the meal. You can keep the rest for a day or so when it will still be very good.

Insalata di Mare
SEAFOOD SALAD

A variety of fish can appear in this salad, preferably a shell-fish of some kind, and some prawns or shrimps. Squid, cuttlefish or octopus is the essential ingredient, for both looks and texture. All should be very fresh – frozen will not do. Look in your market for inspiration.

SERVES 4

500 g/1 lb mussels in their shells
350 g/12 oz squid
150 g/5 oz giant prawns (jumbo shrimp)
2 scallops weighing about 120 g/about 4 oz without shells
the juice of 1 lemon
3 tbsp olive oil
salt and freshly ground black pepper
1 tbsp chopped parsley
a small bunch of chives, chopped

Scrub the mussels thoroughly, discarding any that are open or have broken shells. Put a wine glass of water in a saucepan with a lid, add the mussels and steam them over a strong flame for a minute or two. Cool, and then remove the mussels from their shells. Clean the squid by removing the translucent bone and cutting off the head. Keep the tentacles whole in bunches and do not cut the body at this point.

Bring a saucepan of water to the boil and add some salt. Put in the squid, the prawns and the scallops. The cooking time should not take more than 10–15 minutes: remove the prawns after 5 minutes; the squid, too (if they are small ones), will be cooked in 5 minutes. Test for tenderness and drain the fish when cooked. Cut the scallops in half and large squid into 1.5 cm/¾ in slices. Cut the prawns into four. Mix in the mussels. Dress with the lemon juice and olive oil, season with salt, pepper and parsley and scatter the chives over the top.

INSALATA DI MARE

LE PERNICI CON LE PERE

One of the best game birds is the partridge. With its delicate flavour, it is an excellent autumnal dish. In my restaurant I serve it in the simplest way possible: roasted in the oven and accompanied by a pear in sweet-and-sour syrup. The pears can, naturally, be prepared well in advance, as they are served cold. I would recommend that you make a few extra ones and keep them for use at a later date.

SERVES 4

4 partridges, ready larded if possible, plus giblets
salt and freshly ground black pepper
60 g/good 2 oz/4 tbsp butter
1 tbsp brandy
1 ladleful of stock

FOR THE PEARS:
2 not-too-ripe pears
1 small wineglass of water
1 small wineglass of wine vinegar
100 g/4 oz/½ cup sugar
10 cloves
4 grates of nutmeg
2 cm/¾ in stick cinnamon

First prepare the pears. Peel them, halve them and remove the seeds. Place in a saucepan the water, vinegar, sugar and spices, and bring to the boil. Immerse the pears in this liquid and cook for 15 minutes, depending on their texture: by the end of this time the pears should still be quite firm. Allow to cool.

Remove the liver and giblets from the partridges and put them to one side. Salt and pepper the partridges inside and out.

Preheat the oven to 200°C/400°F/gas mark 6. Take a casserole, heat it thoroughly on the stove and then add half the butter. Place the four partridges and their giblets in the pan and fry over a high flame for 5 minutes on all three sides and 5 minutes on their backs. Throw away the larding and take out the giblets and liver, which should now be cooked. Replace the partridges in the same pan together with the second half of the butter, the brandy and stock, and roast in the oven for 15–20 minutes. When cooked, remove the partridges and keep them warm while you make the sauce. Use the partridge juices to make the sauce: purée the liver and giblets and stir into the roasting juices over a low flame, then season with salt and pepper. Serve the partridges with the pears and a little sauce.

Broccoli allo Zenzero

BROCCOLI WITH GINGER

Another recipe traditionally served in my restaurant. Both the broccoli and the ginger should be fresh.

SERVES 4

500 g/1 lb broccoli heads
2 cloves garlic
a piece of ginger the size of a walnut
4 tbsp olive oil
salt and freshly ground black pepper

Wash the broccoli and separate into florets. Slice the garlic; peel the ginger and cut it into thin strips.

Boil the broccoli in salted water until cooked al dente, then drain. Heat the oil and fry the garlic and ginger together for a few minutes, taking care not to let the garlic brown. Pour over the broccoli and serve.

PASTIERA DI GRANO

PASTIERA DI GRANO

WHEAT TART

In Naples, Easter isn't Easter without this wonderful tart. It has, apparently, very old origins and it symbolizes wealth. Grain and ricotta cheese are the most basic of foods, and if you do not have them, it means you are very poor. The important ingredient for it is whole wheat grain, which can even be bought in cans precisely for this purpose. It is called Gran Pastiera, made by Chirico, and is obtainable from Italian food shops.

SERVES 10 OR MORE

FOR THE PASTRY:
300 g/10 oz/2 cups flour
150 g/5 oz/³⁄₄ cup caster (superfine) sugar
150 g/5 oz/²⁄₃ cup butter
3 large egg yolks

FOR THE FILLING:
200 g/7 oz whole wheat to be soaked, or a 440 g/15 oz can of cooked wheat
500 ml/17 fl oz/2 cups milk (if you are soaking your own whole wheat)
the grated rind of ½ lemon and ½ orange
1 tsp powdered cinnamon
2 tsp vanilla sugar
300 g/10 oz/1¼ cups ricotta cheese
4 large eggs, separated
1 small wineglass orange-flower water
150 g/5 oz/³⁄₄ cup candied peel, chopped
225 g/8 oz/1 cup plus 2 tbsp caster (superfine) sugar

The grain needs to be soaked for 24 hours then simmered in the milk with the grated lemon rind for 3–4 hours on a very low heat. When it is cooked, add the cinnamon, vanilla sugar and the orange rind. Cool and keep until the next day. Alternatively, use the canned ready-cooked grain, and add the above including lemon rind.

Make the pastry by working together the sugar, butter and the egg yolks until smooth, then add the flour and make a smooth dough. Put aside in a cool place for 1 hour or more. Preheat the oven to 190°C/375°F/gas mark 5.

To make the filling, beat the ricotta with the egg yolks and the orange-flower water. Add the candied peel and the flavoured grain to the ricotta mixture. Beat the egg whites with the caster sugar and fold them very gently into the ricotta. Butter a large flan tin 31 cm/12 in in diameter. Press two-thirds of the pastry into the flan tin, covering the bottom and sides with an equal thickness. Pour in the filling. Roll out the remaining pastry and cut into long strips to form a lattice top to the tart. Put in the oven and bake for 45 minutes. Allow to cool and dust with icing (confectioners') sugar.

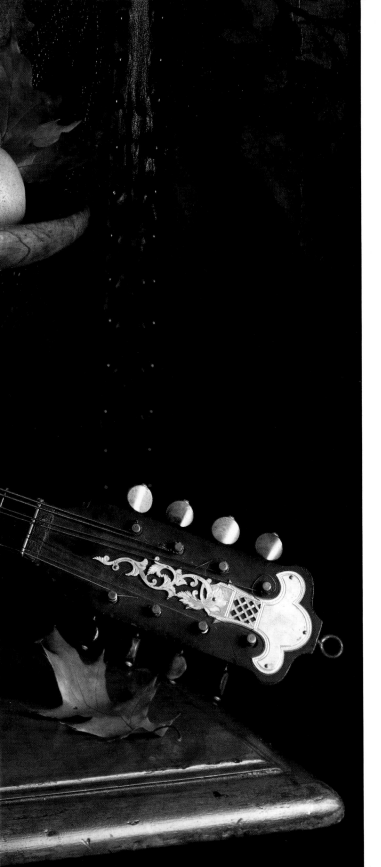

MENU 12

*M*uch as I love the wonderful wild mushrooms that I pick from late summer through to early winter, the morel – a springtime mushroom – is one of my absolute favourites. It can be scarce in some years, but fortunately it reconstitutes perfectly from dried, and so can be used at any time to accompany superb dishes such as these *gnocchi*. Duck with mango – a superb pairing of rich meat with slightly acidic fruit – is always in demand at Neal Street, and so is the hazelnut crunch which we sell in our food shop next door.

LEFT: GNOCCHI CON SPUGNOLE

GNOCCHI CON SPUGNOLE

GNOCCHI WITH MORELS

Morels have only a short growing season, but since they dry particularly well, you can use them at any time of the year. I made this dish with dried ones, and the result was stunning: the combination of Italian gnocchi (the famous potato and flour dumplings) with just a hint of creamy sauce and the delicious morel makes a very succulent dish indeed.

SERVES 4

FOR THE GNOCCHI:
900 g/2 lb floury potatoes, cooked and mashed while still warm
200 g/7 oz/1⅓ cups flour
pinch of salt

FOR THE SAUCE
40 g/1½ oz dried morels
2 shallots, chopped
45 g/1½ oz/3 tbsp butter
1 x 400 g/14 oz can peeled plum tomatoes, finely chopped
150 ml/5 fl oz/⅔ cup double (heavy) cream
salt and pepper
50 g/2 oz/¼ cup freshly grated Parmesan cheese

Soak the morels in lukewarm water for 20 minutes, or until soft and spongy, while you make the gnocchi. Knead the mashed potatoes on a work surface, adding the flour gradually until you obtain a soft but elastic dough. With your hands roll the dough into a series of 2 cm/¾ in diameter cylinders (sprinkle with flour to prevent sticking). Slice the cylinders of dough into chunks 3 cm/1¼ in long. Hold a large (preferably wooden) fork in your left hand, prongs down, and use your thumb to squeeze the chunks of dough against the prongs, one at a time, letting the gnocchi roll off on to a clean cloth. They should curl up like ribbed shells as they roll off the fork.

For the sauce, drain the morels well. Fry the chopped shallots in the butter until golden, add the morels and the chopped tomatoes and cook for a further 5 minutes. Stir in the cream and add salt and pepper to taste.

Cook the gnocchi in plenty of salted water: they are ready when they start to float to the surface. Scoop them out, drain well and mix with the sauce. Sprinkle with Parmesan cheese and serve.

PETTO D'ANITRA AL MANGO

DUCK WITH MANGO

It is quite usual to see duck accompanied by some sort of fruit – be it cherries, grapes, dates or, of course, oranges – in recipes that seem mostly to be of French origin. I do not wish to start heated discussions with our French friends, but 'le canard à l'orange' was a dish served up in the Tuscan courts in 1600 – a fact upheld by several menus from that period.

I have preferred to use mango (all the better if it is not totally ripe), as it adds a touch of acidity to the duck meat which is usually rather fatty. This is another favourite dish in my restaurant where whole ducks are used (for obvious reasons). This gives us the additional advantage of obtaining an excellent demi-glace of duck which will be used later as a sauce. However, if you are preparing this recipe at home I suggest you use only the duck breast, one per portion.

SERVES 4

4 duck breasts (breast halves) with their skin
salt and freshly ground black pepper
60 g/a good 2 oz/4 tbsp butter
3 or 4 tbsp stock
1 large mango (not too ripe)
2 tsp brandy
1 tbsp mango chutney
1 tsp potato starch

Salt and pepper the duck breasts. Heat half of the butter in a heavy pan which has a fitting lid, and quickly fry the breasts, skin-side down, for 5 or 6 minutes. Turn the duck breasts over, add the stock, cover with the lid and cook for a further 10 minutes, lowering the heat slightly.

Meanwhile, cut the mango in two halves, peel off the skin and cut the flesh from the stone in thin slices. When the breasts are cooked, remove them from the pan and keep warm.

Put the pan back on a moderate heat and add the remaining butter. Stir it well into the duck juices and add the brandy, the mango chutney and some salt and pepper. Cook for a moment, then stir in the potato starch, mixed to a paste in a little of the sauce.

To serve, cut the duck breasts slantwise into slices and arrange them on warm plates alternating with slices of fresh mango. Pour a little of the sauce over the breasts and serve.

FINOCCHI GRATINATI

FENNEL AU GRATIN

It is a pity that this most delicious dish, very well known and appreciated in Italy, is hardly known abroad. It has a very distinctive flavour and can accompany both meat and fish. Choose round, fat, firm bulbs of fennel.

SERVES 6

1 kg/2 lb fennel bulbs
45 g/1½ oz/3 tbsp butter
salt and freshly ground black pepper
20 g/scant 1 oz/¼ cup dry bread crumbs

Wash and clean the whole fennel bulbs. Cut off the top stalks and the hard base, and cut each bulb in two lengthwise.

Preheat the oven to 200°C/400°F/gas mark 6. Boil the fennel halves in salted water for 15 minutes, drain and leave to cool a bit before slicing. Butter an ovenproof dish, slice the fennel into 1 cm/½ in slices and lay them in the dish, slightly overlapping each slice. Dot with pieces of butter, season with salt and pepper, and sprinkle over the breadcrumbs. Bake in the oven for 15–20 minutes until brown and crispy.

CROCCANTE DI NOCCIOLE

HAZELNUT CRUNCH

Almost every Christmas, I make this sweet and put it into little individual cellophane bags to give as presents to friends and relations. A little care is needed when making them, as the liquid sugar used to make the hazelnuts stick together is extremely hot and will mean many a burnt finger!

MAKES 1.25 KG/3 LB HAZELNUT CRUNCH

700 g/1½ lb hazelnuts, shelled
peel of ½ lemon and ½ orange
700 g/1½ lb sugar
6 tbsp good-quality honey
about 10 sheets of rice paper
a lemon half

Preheat the oven to 230°C/450°F/gas mark 8.

Put the hazelnuts in a flat ovenproof pan and roast in a hot oven until the skins remove easily and the hazelnuts remain pale in colour. Cut the lemon and orange peel into fine strips, and then into cubes. Put the sugar in a heavy-bottomed pan along with the honey on a medium to strong flame. Stirring most of the time, cook until the sugar and honey have become liquid and turn brown in colour. This takes about 10 minutes. At this point add the peel and the nuts to the caramel in the pan. Stir, keeping the pan on the heat until all the nuts are well coated. Remove from the heat. Make little heaps of the hazelnut caramel on the sheets of rice paper using 3–4 tablespoons for each heap. The nuts tend to stick up from the caramel: wait till you reach the bottom of the pan and use the remaining caramel to fill up any gaps around the nuts. Flatten the heaps by patting down with half a lemon. Leave to cool a bit, but when still warm, cut with a large knife into 2 x 3 cm (1 x 1½ in) pieces: if the caramel is cold the knife will shatter rather than cut the pieces. Store in airtight jars.

A totally Sicilian menu that begins with spaghetti with wonderful *bottargà* (dried mullet roe from Sicily or Sardinia), followed by tuna fish stewed in the Sicilian style, with garlic, tomatoes, herbs and black olives, and concludes with a speciality dessert from the island called *cannoli.* The result is a memorable feast full of happy, sunny flavours.

SPAGHETTI CON BOTTARGA

SPAGHETTI WITH BOTTARGA

Bottarga is a typically Sardinian and Sicilian speciality. It merely consists of mullet roe – eggs that have been dried and salted, resulting in something like a dry caviar! As it is rather difficult to come by abroad, I always try to buy up a quantity when I am in Italy, as it keeps for some time. These dried eggs are simply grated over the cooked pasta, and give it a very distinctive flavour.

SERVES 4

400 g/14 oz thick spaghetti
50 g/2 oz/4 tbsp butter
1 small dried hot red chilli pepper (or 2 if you like), finely chopped
50 g/2 oz bottarga
salt and freshly ground black pepper

Cook the spaghetti for about 15 minutes or until it is al dente, then drain. Melt some butter over it and sprinkle with some dried chilli pepper. Serve on preheated dishes and grate the bottarga over the pasta. Season with black pepper and salt – taking into account, of course, that the bottarga will itself be very salty.

It is essential that you grate the bottarga over the spaghetti only seconds before serving.

TONNO ALLA SICILIANA
TUNA SICILIAN STYLE

Tuna fish is commonly found in Sicily and its meat is very substantial and is usually cut into slices so that it can be either fried, grilled or, as in this typical recipe, stewed.

SERVES 4

4 fresh tuna steaks, weighing about 200 g/7 oz each
salt
flour for dusting
4 tbsp olive oil

FOR THE SAUCE:
1 red sweet pepper, cut into strips
2 cloves garlic, chopped finely
4 tomatoes, skinned and chopped
20 black olives
2 bay leaves and a sprig of rosemary
a pinch of dried oregano
1 dried hot chilli pepper
1 small glass of dry Marsala
freshly ground black pepper

Salt the steaks and then dust them with flour on both sides.

Heat the olive oil in a large frying pan and, when hot, fry the steaks briefly on both sides. Remove them from the pan and reduce the heat. Put the red peppers in the frying pan, then add the garlic. Add the tomatoes, olives, rosemary, bay leaves, oregano and crushed chilli. Then add the Marsala and return the tuna to the sauce. Simmer gently for 15–20 minutes with the lid on the pan, season with black pepper and serve.

FAGIOLINI AL BURRO E PANGRATTATO
FRENCH (GREEN) BEANS AND BREADCRUMBS

Make your own fresh breadcrumbs for this delicious way of serving green beans. The crunchiness of the breadcrumbs combined with the tender beans is a surprising texture.

SERVES 4

100 g/4 oz/2 cups fresh breadcrumbs
300 g/10 oz French (green) beans, topped and tailed
100 g/4 oz/½ cup butter
salt and freshly ground black pepper

Preheat the oven to 230°C/450°F/gas mark 8.

Crumble the bread into coarse crumbs, best done in a food processor, where you can use both the crust and the crumbs. Lay the crumbs in an oven tin and bake for 5–6 minutes. They should become golden, not brown.

Drop the beans in boiling salted water and cook until al dente. Meanwhile, melt the butter in a small frying pan. When fizzing, add the toasted breadcrumbs and stir until they have soaked up the butter and turned a lovely brown. Season with salt and pepper. Cover the boiled beans with the breadcrumb mixture. This is an excellent recipe to go with chicken or fish.

RIGHT: CANNOLI ALLA SICILIANA

CANNOLI ALLA SICILIANA

SICILIAN CANNOLI

This is a very typical Sicilian speciality using, once again, ricotta cheese. To shape the cannoli you need four or five cylinders 2.5 cm/1 in in diameter and 15 cm/6 in long. In Italy they use lengths of bamboo cane, and they also sell the equivalent in tin. If you ever go to Italy, don't forget to buy some of these moulds.

MAKES 10 CANNOLI

FOR THE PASTRY:
25 g/1 oz/2 tbsp butter
25 g/1 oz/2 tbsp caster (superfine) sugar
3½ tbsp dry white wine
2 tbsp vanilla sugar
a pinch of salt
150 g/5 oz/1 cup flour
1 beaten egg for sealing the cannoli
plenty of lard for deep frying

FOR THE FILLING:
500 g/1 lb/2½ cups very fresh ricotta cheese
100 g/4 oz/½ cup caster (superfine) sugar
1 tbsp vanilla sugar
2 tbsp orange-flower water
50 g/2 oz candied lemon peel
50 g/2 oz candied orange peel
50 g/2 oz glacé cherries
50 g/2 oz candied angelica
80 g/3 oz bittersweet chocolate
icing (confectioners') sugar for dusting

Beat the butter and sugar together until light and creamy. Add the wine, vanilla sugar and salt and mix together. Fold in the flour and knead a bit to form a dough. Put the dough aside in a cool place for at least 2 hours.

Roll out the dough with a rolling pin to a large sheet 3 mm/⅛ in thick. Cut the sheet into 10 cm/4 in squares. Place a bamboo cane diagonally across one square of pastry and wrap the two opposite corners around the cane to form the cannoli. Seal the join by moistening the pastry with egg. Make three or four at a time (this number will probably be dictated by the number of cannoli moulds you have).

Now heat the lard in a large deep pan: the lard must be deep enough to cover the cannoli. When the lard is very hot, carefully put the cannoli in to fry. I find a long-pronged cooking fork is the best implement for handling the cannoli in the boiling lard. The cannoli are cooked when they have turned golden brown. This will only take 1½–2 minutes. The pastry will puff up as it cooks, so the cannoli have a plump tube shape when ready. Lay the cannoli on kitchen paper towel to drain. Only remove the metal tubes or bamboo cane when the cannoli are cool.

To make the filling, beat the ricotta cheese with a fork, then add the sugar, vanilla sugar and orange-flower water. The ricotta should become creamier in consistency. Cut the peel, glacé cherries and angelica into small pieces. Chop the chocolate and mix these ingredients into the ricotta mixture. Fill each cannoli with the ricotta mixture and line up on a plate. Dust with icing (confectioners') sugar and serve cool, but do not refrigerate.

A Moscato Passito di Pantelleria is the correct dessert wine to accompany this very delicious sweet.

We head back north with this menu, which is typically hearty food to bring a warm glow when the weather is cold. Most of the main ingredients featured here are nearing their peak in the last month or two of the year, especially the pheasant, and the bitter salad leaves enhanced by peppery rocket/arugula. For a change, I suggest a creamy cheese instead of the more usual sweet dessert.

ZUPPA DI FAGIANO AL PORTO
PHEASANT SOUP WITH PORT

This is a soup that has an intense, gamey flavour and is particularly appropriate during the autumn hunting season when a variety of game is on the market. Whenever I serve roast pheasant, I always take care to keep the leftovers and the cooking juices, which form the basis of an exceptional soup.

SERVES 4

FOR THE STOCK:
1 medium-sized onion, chopped
2 tbsp olive oil
1 carrot, cut in pieces
2 celery stalks, chopped
scraps and leftovers of pheasant or other game
about 1 litre/1¾ pt/1 qt water
a nut of butter and a little flour
2 tbsp double (heavy) cream
1 glass of port
salt and freshly ground black pepper
croûtons or white truffle (optional)

Fry the chopped onion gently in the oil until golden brown. Add to this the chopped carrot and celery and the scraps of meat and bone. Pour in enough water to cover all these ingredients, and leave to simmer for about 1½ hours.

Strain the stock through a sieve. Melt the butter and mix into it the flour, the cream and the port. Add the stock and reheat gently. Salt and pepper to taste and serve with either some croûtons or a couple of slices of white truffle.

FEGATO ALLA VENEZIANA

CALF'S LIVER VENETIAN STYLE

This typical Venetian recipe has become a classic Italian dish which can be found on the menu of any good Italian restaurant. The combination of liver and onions is delicious.

SERVES 4

300 g/10 oz onions
4 tbsp olive oil
400 g/14 oz calf's liver, sliced into thin strips
flour for coating
salt and freshly ground black pepper
2 tbsp wine vinegar
1 tbsp finely chopped parsley

Coarsely slice the onions and fry in the olive oil in a wide pan. Slowly cook the onions until they become translucent, but do not let them burn. When they are cooked, remove the onions from the pan and put them aside while you cook the liver. Coat the pieces of liver in flour and shake off the excess, then fry in the same pan over a medium flame, turning frequently. Return the onions to the pan. Season with salt and pepper and then add the wine vinegar, which should be left to reduce a little. Serve with a sprinkling of parsley.

RIGHT: ZUPPA DI FAGIANO AL PORTO

CICORIA E RADICCHIO CON RUCOLA

CHICORY (BELGIAN ENDIVE) AND RADICCHIO
WITH ROCKET (ARUGULA) SALAD

The combination of slightly bitter flavours here produces a very appetizing salad.

In Italy the green chicory is used, cut very thinly. You can also use the white Belgian type, thus achieving a very Italian colour effect – the white of the chicory, the red of the radicchio and the green of the rocket.

SERVES 4

200 g/7 oz chicory (Belgian endive)
300 g/10 oz radicchio
100 g/4 oz fresh rocket (arugula)
the juice of 1 lemon
4 tbsp olive oil
salt and freshly ground black pepper

After washing and drying the salad ingredients, cut the chicory and radicchio into strips and mix with the rocket. Serve dressed with an oil and lemon vinaigrette.

RICOTTA RIFATTA

REMADE RICOTTA

This is created by putting two different cheeses together – ricotta and gorgonzola. These two cheeses complement each other perfectly, with the rough texture of the ricotta and the sharp taste of the gorgonzola. If you add some finely chopped parsley you will obtain an excellent creamy dessert cheese. Accompany with fresh celery stalks.

SERVES 8

100 g/4 oz gorgonzola, cut in small pieces
3 tbsp milk
400 g/14 oz/2 cups ricotta (preferably made with sheep's milk)
2 tbsp finely chopped parsley
500 g/1 lb celery stalks, cleaned

Mix the gorgonzola quite thoroughly with the milk. (If the gorgonzola you buy is very blue and strong, use a slightly smaller proportion of it.)

Now break up the ricotta cheese and add it to the gorgonzola mixture. Beat together until you have a creamy texture. Add the chopped parsley and arrange on a serving dish. Decorate the top with a fork and serve with celery stalks.

LEFT: CICORIA E RADICCHIO CON RUCOLA

*T*o conclude our culinary concert, I have selected two more classic dishes, namely the famous minestrone soup and the equally well-known dessert called *zabaglione,* which I like to enrich with a little sweet *moscato* wine. Venison, and all other game, are very popular with Italians, and for me the best way to serve the steaks is with wild mushrooms.

I hope that you have enjoyed these feasts from my country and the superb music. Music and food are two inseparable parts of our cultural life and the sharing of both with good company and in the right atmosphere will be greatly beneficial for your body, mind and soul.

MINESTRONE

*T*his soup is so well known throughout the world that it is certainly not necessary for me to give a translation. The name derives from 'minestra', meaning a soup. (In many parts of Italy minestra means green.) Normally this is prepared with whatever leftover vegetables are to be found in the kitchen.

Perhaps the most practical hint for you to follow (and which will immediately transform even the dullest of vegetables) is that the fine flavour of Parma ham is essential to the success of this dish.

SERVES 4

8 tbsp olive oil
1 small onion, chopped
a good 250 g/9 oz prosciutto scraps
1.5 litres/3 pt/1½ qt water
a total of 1.5 kg/3 lb vegetables, made up of any or all of the following: carrots, celery, courgettes (zucchini), cauliflower, potatoes, fresh peas, beetroot (beet), garlic, leeks, Brussels sprouts, parsnips, marrows (squash)
1 x 400 g/14 oz can borlotti beans (if you can find fresh ones, so much the better)
2 small tomatoes, skinned
some fresh basil leaves, or 1 tsp dried basil
4 tbsp freshly grated Parmesan cheese

Heat the oil in a large saucepan. First fry the chopped onion, then add the prosciutto pieces and the water and let this simmer for an hour. Meanwhile, clean the vegetables and chop into cubes. Discard the prosciutto pieces and add the vegetables of your choice, as well as the drained beans. Add the skinned tomatoes after a further 20 minutes. Cook for at least a further 30 minutes. Then add the basil and serve piping hot. Minestrone is also a delicacy when eaten cold. Freshly grated Parmesan should be served separately.

Camoscio in Salmi

VENISON STEAK WITH WILD MUSHROOMS

This is a typical dish of the Aosta Valley region where it is still possible to hunt deer with a licence that is rather hard to come by. In the rest of Europe it is much easier than in Italy to come across this king of the mountains; in America it is easier still.

The recipe requires that you marinate the meat for a long time in a rather complex marinade. This is to take away the too intense gamey flavour of the meat and to make it more tender. It is traditional to serve the venison with polenta, which turns it into a princely dish.

SERVES 4

4 x 1 cm/½ in thick slices from a venison leg or fillet, weighing
a total of 600 g/1¼ lb
flour for dusting

FOR THE MARINADE:
1 litre/¾ pt/1 qt good red wine
1 small onion, chopped
5 bay leaves
1 sprig of rosemary
2 cloves of garlic, chopped
2 carrots, chopped

2 celery stalks, chopped
1 sprig of thyme
5 cloves
10 juniper berries
1 tbsp split black peppercorns
salt

FOR THE SAUCE:
45 g/1½ oz/3 tbsp butter
1 small onion, sliced
100 g/4 oz smoked bacon, chopped
350 g/12 oz mushrooms, sliced

Marinate the venison for 3 days before you are to cook the dish.

Take the meat from the marinade, keeping the marinade to add to the sauce later, and dry with a cloth. Lightly dust the slices with flour and then fry for 5 minutes in the butter until brown on each side, and put aside to keep hot. Then, in the same butter, fry the sliced onion and the smoked bacon cut into small pieces. Now add the sliced mushrooms and fry all together for a few minutes until golden. Add 2 glasses of the strained marinade and allow to bubble and reduce briefly. Add the venison pieces, coat with the sauce and serve.

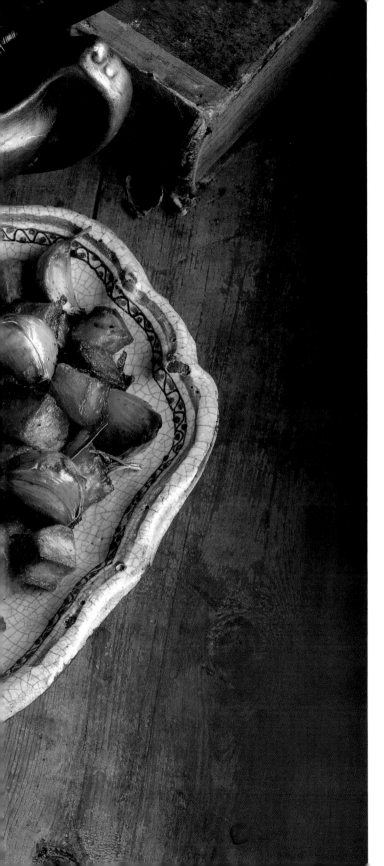

Patate Fritte con Aglio e Rosmarino

FRIED POTATOES WITH GARLIC AND ROSEMARY

This is another wonderful recipe containing simple but effective ingredients. The combination of rosemary and garlic gives an unmistakably Italian flavour.

Serves 4

500 g/1 lb peeled potatoes
8 tbsp olive oil
8 large cloves garlic, unpeeled
1 sprig of fresh rosemary
salt and freshly ground black pepper

Cut the potatoes into cubes 1.5 cm/¾ in square. Heat the olive oil in a large frying pan and when hot add the potato cubes. Spread them out in the pan, but do not stir until they form a golden crust. Turn the potatoes over and add the unpeeled garlic. Fry together to brown on all sides. Just before the end add the rosemary, salt and pepper.

LEFT: CAMOSCIO IN SALMI WITH PATATE FRITTE CON AGLIO E ROSMARINO

ZABAGLIONE AL MOSCATO
ZABAGLIONE WITH MUSCATEL

Zabaglione is one of the best-known Italian desserts. You will find this delicious sweet, based on eggs, in nearly every Italian restaurant, both in Italy and abroad. Marsala wine is normally used along with the sugar to produce the fluffy consistency. The use of a good Moscato Passito instead of Marsala gives it a fresh flavour. If you don't have a special round copper pan, you can use a round bowl set over a large pan of hot water.

SERVES 4

4 medium egg yolks
100 g/4 oz/½ cup caster (superfine) sugar
170 ml/6 fl oz/¾ cup Moscato Passito

Beat the egg yolks with the sugar until the sugar is dissolved. Add the wine and beat for a few minutes more. Put the bowl in the bain marie over a low heat and, using a whisk, beat until a firm, foamy consistency is obtained. Pour into individual glasses and serve with very delicately flavoured biscuits (cookies).

RIGHT: ZABAGLIONE AL MOSCATO

INDEX

ACKNOWLEDGEMENTS

Food photography by Laurie Evans

THE BRIDGEMAN ART LIBRARY:
p1 & 32 *The Wedding Feast* by Sandro Botticelli (1444/5-1510)/Private Collection; p10 *Summer* (detail) by Guiseppe Arcimboldo (1527-93) (school of)/Ex Edward James Foundation, Sussex; p16 *The Young Bacchus*, c. 1591-3 by Michelangelo Merisi da Caravaggio (1571-1610)/Galleria degli Uffizi, Florence; p21 *Still Life* (detail) by Michelangelo Merisi da Caravaggio (1571-1610)/Private Collection; p27 CRL23.459 *Summer*, 1573 by Guiseppe Arcimboldo (1527-93)/Louvre, Paris/Lauros-Giraudon; p37 *The Sick Bacchus* (detail) by Michelangelo Merisi da Caravaggio (1571-1610)/Galleria Borghese, Rome; p42 *Still Life of Raspberries,* *Lemons and Asparagus* by Italian School (18th Century)/Gavin Graham Gallery, London; p46 *Still Life of Fruit* by Italian School (17th Century)/Rafael Valls Gallery, London; p52 Winter by Guiseppe Arcimboldo (1527-93)/Ex-Edward James Foundation, Sussex; p57 *Basket with Fruit,* c.1596 (detail) by Michelangelo Merisi da Caravaggio (1571-1610)/Ambrosiana, Milan; p62 *Still Life of Fish* by Guiseppe Recco (1634-95)/Galleria degli Uffizi, Florence; p69 *Two Wild Ducks Hanging* by Cesare Dandini (c.1595-1658)/Galleria degli Uffizi, Florence; p73 *Still Life of Cherries, Marrows and Pears* (detail) by Italian School (18th Century)/Gavin Graham Gallery, London; p77 *Still Life* by Giovanni-Battista Rouppolo or Ruopolo (1629-93)/Private Collection; p82 *The Supper at Emmaus* (detail) by Michelangelo Merisi da Caravaggio (1571-1610)/National Gallery, London.